INTENTIONAL LIVING

INTENTIONAL LIVING

Eight steps to leading an infinitely fulfilling life

Jayne Wallace

BLOOMSBURY
LONDON · OXFORD · NEW YORK · NEW DELHI · SYDNEY

BLOOMSBURY PUBLISHING
Bloomsbury Publishing Plc
50 Bedford Square, London, WC1B 3DP, UK
Bloomsbury Publishing Ireland Limited,
29 Earlsfort Terrace, Dublin 2, D02 AY28, Ireland

BLOOMSBURY, BLOOMSBURY PUBLISHING and the Diana logo
are trademarks of Bloomsbury Publishing Plc

First published in Great Britain 2025

Copyright © Jayne Wallace, 2025

Jayne Wallace is identified as the author of this work in accordance with the
Copyright, Designs and Patents Act 1988.

Text from *The Mythic Goddess Tarot* by Jayne Wallace © CICO Books

All rights reserved. No part of this publication may be: i) reproduced or
transmitted in any form, electronic or mechanical, including photocopying,
recording or by means of any information storage or retrieval system without
prior permission in writing from the publishers; or ii) used or reproduced in
any way for the training, development or operation of artificial intelligence (AI)
technologies, including generative AI technologies. The rights holders expressly
reserve this publication from the text and data mining exception as per Article
4(3) of the Digital Single Market Directive (EU) 2019/790

Bloomsbury Publishing Plc does not have any control over, or responsibility for,
any third-party websites referred to in this book. All internet addresses given in
this book were correct at the time of going to press. The author and publisher
regret any inconvenience caused if addresses have changed or sites have ceased to
exist, but can accept no responsibility for any such changes

A catalogue record for this book is available from the British Library

ISBN: HB: 978-1-5266-8283-3; eBook: 978-1-5266-8279-6;
ePDF: 978-1-5266-8280-2

2 4 6 8 10 9 7 5 3 1

Typeset by Ed Pickford

Printed and bound in Great Britain by CPI Group (UK) Ltd, Croydon CR0 4YY

To find out more about our authors and books visit
www.bloomsbury.com and sign up for our newsletters

For product safety related questions contact productsafety@bloomsbury.com

CONTENTS

Introduction   1

EMPOWERMENT

Step 1: Confidence and How to Keep Hold of It   11
Step 2: Learning to Listen to Your Gut Instinct   34
Step 3: Finding and Setting Boundaries   56
Step 4: Finding Your Potential   83

ENLIGHTENMENT

Step 5: Your Inner Goddess   113
Step 6: Recharge and Embrace Rest   134
Step 7: Finding Your Self   162
Step 8: How to Be Grateful   185

Jayne's Spiritual Kit Bag   201

INTRODUCTION

Welcome, friend.

Thank you for joining me here. Tell me: what is it you are searching for?

Do you wish to empower aspects of your life and yourself but don't know where to start?

Are you looking for answers without being sure of the questions?

Do you search for insight, peace and strength in every day?

Are you ready to join me on a spiritual journey of self-discovery?

If so, you have come to the right place.

This book is the realisation of a particular dream for me, born from a life of psychic work and understanding through my clients and my own personal practices. These experiences have become the foundation and inspiration for my eight-step pilgrimage to a more intentional way of living, taking thoroughly modern issues and giving spiritual answers and advice. I don't think there has been a better time to share what I know and help where I can.

You may be a strong believer in spirituality, or curious about what it could mean to you, or perhaps you are a doubter with low expectations, but whatever your motivation for being here, I am glad you are. There are too many struggles to face in life so, if we can connect to something that instils calm and clarity in the everyday, then who wouldn't want to embrace that? From tapping into your spiritual abilities and trusting your gut instinct to co-creating with the universe and establishing reassuring rituals, we can find ways to gain insight, self-knowledge and serenity. It's easier than you may think and more imperative than you realise.

When I was a little girl, I was surrounded by what I thought were imaginary friends. I never felt alone – impossible with seven siblings – but it was a feeling that went beyond the noisy physical presence of my large Essex family. I could sense an energy that was fuelled by angels and auras. At night my dreams were surreal, filled with images of flying to distant lands and seeing things I would not have known about at that age. I knew this was unusual even then, but I was never afraid. At primary school, I once went up to a girl I didn't know and said her dad loved her and he was with her. I could see him as a sort of presence next to her. The teacher was furious with me and wanted to know why I was saying such hurtful things. I didn't know the girl's father had died, I just knew he was with her, and I was too young to stop myself sharing what I saw and felt.

INTRODUCTION

It helped that my mum understood. She told me I had an ability that other people might find hard to accept and took me to a spiritualist church she regularly attended. I was buoyed by the great people there and the incredible amount of love and acceptance in the room. A clairvoyant told me I would be doing this one day and it was a relief to be somewhere that made complete sense, like returning to a country that spoke the same language as me. Then things changed.

From my early teens, I spent a decade in the spiritual wilderness after health issues, problems at school and ill-advised decisions led me away from my calling. I share these stories within the book, as examples to illustrate my own struggles with belief, acceptance and confidence. It wasn't until my mum's death, when I was in my early twenties, that I felt the energy and spirits flood back through the channel I had effectively blocked for over ten years.

I returned to what I knew. Clairvoyancy was my passion, and a skill I spent time working on, before I began to give readings, and it was then that I felt I had truly come home. I took to it like a relieved duck to tranquil water. When I was in my late twenties, I wrote to *Spirit and Destiny* magazine, and they called me in for a meeting. They gave me a column, and that was the final affirmation I needed to know this was all I wanted to do. From then on, the professional part of my spiritual self gained respect, profile and multiple achievements.

As a clairvoyant and the founder of the wellness brand Psychic Sisters, I have been instrumental in the shifting attitude towards spiritualism over the decades. It has been a phenomenal and revolutionary rise. Dismissiveness and cynicism have been joyfully eroded by a rapid hike in interest and a strong belief in a different approach. Now there are high-profile people, large corporations, big brands and foundations who search out meaning in the mystical and talk publicly about their experiences, dispelling some of the myths.

Many years ago, I approached a retailer to ask if they would stock a few of my products. Their response? 'We don't deal with people like you.' Now, we are in Superdrug and ASOS, with a concession in Selfridges since March 2006, and have outlived many established brands. A recent successful investment pitch in *Dragons' Den* has further cemented our position, as has a stack of positive media pieces written about us. I have been lucky to work with an incredible variety of people, including the more well known, like Kim Kardashian, Tracey Emin and Kylie Jenner. Visiting a psychic is seen as a real alternative to therapy and an opportunity to take control of your decisions in a proactive way.

At this point, saying the main reason I do this is to help people sounds like a massive cliché, but it's true. I have an ability, a gift, that I can share for the greater good, and even when I don't try, people who need me find me. Like the woman on the supermarket till who looked straight at me and told me that her mother had died that morning, even though she had not mentioned it to any other customer. Or the passenger next to me on the long-haul flight who had terminal cancer and curled up on the seats with her head in my lap for a session of impromptu healing. I don't ask for these experiences; they come to me, and I am privileged that they do.

INTRODUCTION

When I do a reading, I am like an octopus, with my eight tentacles stretched out to pick up on the energy and feeling in the room. All my senses are activated, I pay attention to the response, I relay messages from the spirits who are present and, if nobody shows up, I convey that too.

I hate the term fortune teller, or the way psychics can be portrayed on television as scarf-wearing, eye-rolling eccentrics possessed by spirits. We are still made fun of and expected to be found at the end of a seaside pier with a crystal ball. Much of my work over the years has been to dispel this image and bring spirituality into the modern world. I travel globally to lecture, and I am a keynote speaker for MENSA. The high-IQ organisation has invited me to speak several times in the USA to share my spiritual journey and how intuition and awareness have benefited me personally and professionally. The first time I did this, the organisers had no idea what turnout to expect for my session and charmingly managed expectations by saying new speakers didn't always pull audiences initially. As we rounded the corner to the lecture room, however, we saw a queue running the length of the corridor and security was called to deal with the number of people who were determined to get into the auditorium.

I have also lectured at the Entrepreneurs' Organization global event in Bahrain to an audience who were keen to understand and embrace a more spiritual approach in business. There is a growing fascination and appetite for looking at our lives from a more spiritual angle.

Clairvoyance is an ability we are all born with, but it needs to be nurtured and protected. Whether it is face-to-face clairvoyant sessions, tarot readings, crystals in our pocket, daily affirmations or taking inspiration from nature, everyone can harness their inner psychic to find confidence, empowerment and wisdom. Let me show you how.

So, now you know why I am here, but why are you?

Have you lost touch with your intuition?

Do you struggle with confidence and boundaries?

Are you keen to learn more about manifestation?

Do you want to connect with your inner goddess?

You are exactly where you need to be.

Our quest will encompass eight heartfelt intentions to an infinitely fulfilling life. The number eight is the most powerful and magical of all numbers, which transforms into the infinity symbol when laid on its side, representing the continual flow of all things. In the first part of the book – Steps 1 to 4 – we focus on gaining empowerment through boosting our self-confidence, learning how to listen to our gut instinct, building boundaries and reaching our potential. The second part – Steps 5 to 8 – leads us to enlightenment by reconnecting with our inner goddess, embracing the power of rest, engendering self-love and learning how to be grateful.

As we tackle some of the issues that weigh us down, we will call on many of my favourite practices, including crystals, colour, breathwork, manifestation, numerology, recognising angels, spirit guides, affirmations, the importance of rituals, and tarot. You will find these spiritual tools at the points in the book where they are relevant, but they are practices that can be used for any number of needs so feel free to adapt them yourself. At the end of each step is a journalling prompt from me to ignite or encourage your thoughts. Jot down what comes into your head, without overthinking what hits the page. This is your time to process what you have read and look into yourself for your true responses. What comes out may surprise you and it will create a record of your thoughts as you move through the book.

Let's bring a dash of magic (one of my favourite words) into our everyday lives and make it part of our routine. If you have a headache, you take an aspirin. Why wouldn't you take a little spirituality for similar reasons, to ease the big and small stresses, work through issues or plan the future? I hope what comes as you transcend each stage ahead aids self-discovery, gives you strength when you need it and stands with you through the difficult times. At the very least, I hope it makes you think, and who knows, it may even change your life.

One final thing before we dive in.

When I wrote this introduction, I took my deck of tarot cards, gave them a good shuffle and thought about my expectations for this book and what I hoped I could help with. I love tarot cards. They sing to me. They are a perfect example of the spirit guide, the reader and the receiver joining together to lay each card like a building block to grow the story. It is also an activity you can do for yourself with the right deck of cards and a book to refer to as a guide.

I asked the question, 'What do we need in order to pursue our intentional life?' and then I pulled one card from the pack.

The Ten of Cups. A powerful card that symbolises finding an emotional balance within and the ability to seek truth and destiny. It tells us to remain strong, positive and calm as we move forward into the future. Let's keep this in our mind's eye for what is ahead.

EMPOWERMENT

Step 1

CONFIDENCE AND HOW TO KEEP HOLD OF IT

I am dyslexic but, as a child growing up in the 1970s, people just assumed I wasn't very clever. While huge strides were being made through research into dyslexia during this time, the news hadn't yet reached my Essex primary school, where I was considered hopeless by many of the teachers, who enjoyed trying to prove this daily. From a young age, I was told I would never achieve anything because I couldn't read properly. As you can imagine, that was a bit of a blow, and I could have easily accepted this as my fate, but I didn't, and this was all thanks to my parents, who refused to let me believe other people's opinions of who I was. My early confidence came from their faith in me, and it was one of the best gifts they ever gave me.

As much as I flailed around in the education system, at home Mum would give me regular pep talks and challenge me to push myself every day in small ways. Like walking to school on my own, which I hated because it meant crossing a field, and yet I can still remember the glowing achievement I felt when I had done it. Or being told by the domestic science teacher that I couldn't cook and returning home to share this latest fail with Mum, only for her to tell me I absolutely could and giving me the ingredients to bake a cake. She instilled in me one of my often-repeated mantras to try, try and try again and taught me coping mechanisms to navigate my school days, including ways to find my inner calm and encouraging me to think outside the box. Just because I was not academic did not mean I wouldn't amount to anything, she would tell me. I just needed to find my 'thing'.

I dread to think what would have happened to me without those positive reinforcements in my childhood and the nurturing of a strong self-belief that stood me in good stead for the future. I know that for every great experience like mine, there are countless others who have not been as lucky, and their self-confidence has been snuffed out long before adulthood. This has adversely shaped their lives, affecting their self-esteem, decision-making and mental health, sometimes with catastrophic results. I often see this in the work I do with people who are looking for answers and want to be equipped to make changes, whether they have never known confidence, or maybe a difficult relationship has chipped away at it, or a significant event suffocated it.

Confidence is the backbone of our existence and, if I could wave a magic wand, it would be the first gift I would bestow for an intentional life, because it brings many wonderful things with it, imbuing us with happiness, success and wellbeing. It is the fuel in our engines.

I am lucky. I don't let anything stop me; even if I feel insecure, I give it my best shot. I banish the thoughts of self-doubt and keep going, unless there are concrete reasons why I shouldn't. I think my confidence beams out of me, like warm sunshine rather than a blinding laser, and it does so consistently, which reflects the belief I hold in myself. It is a superpower, but I do not take it for granted and I always have spiritual tools to fall back on should I need help. Which brings me on to the good news. I believe confidence and self-esteem are skills, which can be learned, practised and honed like any other ability, meaning each of us can wave a magic wand for ourselves, and I want to show you how.

While confidence means having complete trust in something or someone, self-confidence is feeling the same strength of emotion towards ourselves. This is harder than it looks, and it often flummoxes people because while they may not have a problem showing faith in various external aspects of their life – maybe with their partner, their doctor or their religion – the idea of turning this around and believing in themselves seems impossible. They do not think they are worthy or good enough, which brings us on to our reticent friend, self-esteem! This is different to confidence because it is how we measure our value rather than our skills, and it presents another type of minefield to navigate.

Self-confidence and self-esteem do not always go hand in hand. It is possible to have assurance in certain situations yet still dislike the person you are, or to have belief in your own ability but battle with sharing this publicly for fear of being seen as arrogant or superior. Then there's the old favourite, of doing a good job pretending to be confident and masking the self-doubt you carry, like plastering on a full face of make-up to disguise a feature you hate, driving around in a fancy car to promote an image of success that you may not feel you have achieved, or throwing up secretly before you give an assured presentation. There are so many examples, personal crutches or habits we use to support us through the social hazards and emotional pitfalls of life. And while there is a lot of truth in confidence coming as we grow older, it doesn't suddenly turn up one day along with a scattering of grey hairs or cheaper car insurance. I think you must seek it out, make it comfortable and persuade it to stay.

So how can we diagnose low confidence in ourselves and others? Here are some of the indications we may be familiar with.

1. Making excuses: We are all guilty of doing this in small, insignificant ways, but when these grow and shift our behaviour patterns, we need to stop and take notice. Do you regularly cancel social arrangements, steer clear of friends and feel uncomfortable about meeting new people? Do you find reasons to avoid challenges and refuse to step outside of your comfort zone? Has coming up with excuses become a way of life?

2. Anxiety issues: While there are real situations that trigger stress, being anxious is not a permanent state we should reside in. This is one of the most debilitating feelings and creates a vicious circle, needing

confidence to pull us out of it, and yet this is impossible to conjure up in the middle of a panic attack.

3. People pleasing: A terrible spiral of putting others before yourself, more concerned with their reaction to something than your own response to it. There is an assumption that others will judge you and find you wanting. You believe it doesn't matter what you think, it is what everyone else does that is important because you have no confidence in your own ability or opinions.

4. Self-neglect: This can manifest in several ways, including a lack of care in yourself physically and mentally, an inability to look after your surroundings or self-destruction leading to addiction issues. Basically, any way you can cause yourself harm because you do not think you deserve anything good.

5. Unable to accept praise or criticism: It works both ways. Some people struggle with being reprimanded, negatively evaluated or disapproved of. Others would prefer that in the face of being celebrated and admired. Either reaction shows an inability to cope with comments, for better or worse.

6. The blame game: It isn't our fault. Except sometimes it is and being defensive about it is not the way to handle the situation. Owning it and dealing with whatever the fallout is, is the answer.

7. Shame: This is one of the worst emotions of all. It hides in the shadows, feeding off silence, complicity and fear. The only answer to this is to expose it, but this requires a strength and confidence that can't be found down the back of a sofa. This needs careful handling.

8. Your own worst enemy: When you struggle to ask for help, project a pretend persona or are inordinately hard on yourself. Maybe you are a perfectionist. Or you hide yourself in difficult places like unsuitable relationships, a job you hate or a destabilising home life. I think we have all done this at one time or another.

It's quite the list, I know, and there are relatable elements for us all, even if we have a healthy amount of faith in ourselves. Some, however, may find they are immobilised by one or several of these issues. So, where do you sit on the confidence scale? Be truthful in your responses and be kind to yourself in your realisations, because this is your starting point. Whatever place we find ourselves, we all have work to do.

Tell me…

- Are you supremely confident? (If so, do feel free to jump ahead to the next chapter!)

- Do you lack both self-confidence and self-esteem?

- Are you able to be outwardly confident, but are inwardly hard on yourself?

- Do you trust in your ability, but find yourself unable to translate that into everyday life?

- Do your self-confidence and self-esteem desert you at the worst possible moments?

- Do you imagine that those around you have got life sussed and it is just you that seems to make a complete mess of things?

- Do you put on a good show in public, masking the insecurities you carry?

I think that final question will resonate with so many of us. Confidence is the thread that runs through the following chapters of this book as well as our futures, so it is the first crucial step to living a more intentional life. We need to galvanise our strength, self-belief and bravery to be able to make our own decisions and accept that we won't always be right. If we aren't, we need to learn from what has gone wrong and make the necessary changes, because **confidence is as much about saying 'no' as it is about saying 'yes'**. Healthy self-esteem is the foundation for all the bricks we will lay as we travel forwards into the warm light of awakening and abundance.

Ready? Let's begin.

How many times have you been told in your life 'you need to be more confident!', as if you could do this with a click of your fingers? *Oh, silly me*, you think, with more than a hint of sarcasm, *of course, I just need to be more confident. Why didn't I think of this before?!* Being encouraged to do something without the advice and skills needed to achieve it is like being instructed to get on a bicycle for the first time and ordered not to fall off. I want to break down what we all need to build and maintain confidence and dig into my spiritual kit bag for tools that will help you shift your current mindset. The trick is to start with the smallest, simplest steps towards transformation, almost imperceptible movements that do not ask too much of us in one go. As we inch along, distracted by putting one foot in front of another, we suddenly look up and realise the view has changed. We have changed.

Sustaining the glow

I want to start with kindness. We may be able to show this to our family, friends and even strangers, but often the one person we can't give it to is ourselves. Self-compassion is an essential quality in our journey to a better understanding of who we are and how we perceive others. There is no need to dwell on past mistakes, bad patterns of behaviour or memories that bring the residual heat of embarrassment and shame, because this isn't going to get us anywhere. Let it all go or, more importantly, let it all be. That was then and this is now.

We must quieten the negative inner voice which will whine about this being a pointless exercise, tell us how useless we are and attempt to send us back down well-trodden neuro pathways. What it is really saying is that we are not worthy of love, from ourselves or anyone else, and it is wrong. Every time you catch yourself obsessively analysing or overthinking, stop, focus on taking a deep breath in through your nose followed by a slow exhalation out through your mouth and reflect on a key moment when you were fulfilled and happy. Use the memory of this feeling to recreate it and immerse yourself in its protective, sustaining glow against the negative internal muttering. This is a voice that will return again and again, so be ready to slow your breathing and redirect your thoughts. Turning this into a routine response will help break your old pattern of behaviour. Here is a visualisation I use to calm a cluttered mind.

SPIRITUAL TOOL: VISUALISATION

Give your negative inner voice a name which is not yours and does not belong to anyone you know. Next time it speaks, tell it to shut up. You can even do this out loud if you are on your own and won't startle anyone! Direct your naysayer to climb into a box, shut the lid and seal it with duct tape. Now conjure up a happy memory or send your thoughts to sit calmly somewhere you love, maybe a sunny beach or a cosy café.

Finding your yoga

Closely linked to our quest to be kinder to ourselves is the practice of self-care. This is now an often-used phrase and yet I am not sure how many of us are as good as we could be at looking after mind and body. We know what we need physically – a healthy diet, good-quality sleep and regular exercise – and that these three things combined benefit our mental wellbeing, but we also know how hard this can be to maintain. After a long day at work, we may be too tired to go for a run or cook a meal from scratch, and then we stay up too late watching TV, unable to summon the energy to move from the sofa. Of course, there are times when self-care is about hitting the sofa with a pizza to binge-watch a series, and that is also fine – we just can't do it every night. When I feel my equilibrium teetering, I remind myself to find a balance by repeating a favoured mantra: ***Do everything in moderation rather than addiction***.

As important as it is to look after our physical wellbeing, we need to protect our spirit too, creating time and space for ourselves and knowing when we need to take a break from professional and social demands. Don't wait until the point of mental exhaustion; instead, factor in small pitstops every day, to create moments of relief and rejuvenation. I know this is the opposite of a radical, new approach, but if you feel trapped in your head, find yourself stuck on a work issue or are brooding over a personal problem, put the kettle on. It is the quickest, simplest way to step out of a situation and give you a breather. Don't take your tea back to your desk or your phone. If you can, take your mug outside and drink while watching the birds, and if a tricky thought surfaces, imagine a broom sweeping through your mind, clearing out the dust and debris. Five minutes can be enough time to break a thought process, which means you may be able to return to the problem with a fresh perspective.

There are myriad ways to take time out, giving ourselves permission to carve out an intentional space in our day or week. Maybe it's a long bath, a walk to catch the sunrise or turning off the TV and going to bed with a book. It might be joining a pottery class, booking a massage or organising a weekend away. I call this 'finding your yoga' – as in, discovering your zen place, which could actually be yoga, of course, but then again it may not. My 'yoga' is to walk through the fields near my house (which I realise is ironic considering my aversion to doing this when I was a child) to a log which has been hollowed out as a bench. I sit in the middle of nature, surrounded by ancient trees, watching the wildlife around me. Or I get creative, making wax melts, oils and candles for my business. I know it's technically work, but it's the sort of meditative focus I love. (I look at self-care in more depth in Step 6, page 134.)

> **SPIRITUAL TOOL: FIND YOUR YOGA**
>
> Amidst the hustle and bustle of life, it is important to seek out a peaceful activity which provides escape and fulfilment. For some this is exercise; for others like me, it is being immersed in nature; for a friend of mine, it is a jigsaw puzzle. She sets the puzzle up at one end of her kitchen table and wanders over to it when she puts the kettle on, while dinner is in the oven, after a long day at work or on a lazy Sunday morning. There is no deadline for her to finish it; it is less about the completion of the picture than it is about the process of getting there. It stops her scrolling on her phone and lowers her stress levels, because it stimulates both sides of the brain and gives her bursts of dopamine as the pieces begin to fit. Of course, it can also be seen as an apt metaphor for the challenge of finding things in our brain and putting them together to see the bigger picture of life.

Goals to greatness

Once in a while it is good to get out of our comfort zone and try something new that challenges us in all the right ways. The point is, small or big, there are times when we should put ourselves first and do something that will fill our depleted stores of energy and requires us to be proactive.

I am a big list-maker, and I love to tick things off once I have done them. It reminds me how much I have achieved in a day, which can be useful when I feel like I have been pushing a heavy load up a steep hill and not getting anywhere. Seeing my accomplishments stops me feeling demoralised and gives me the push I need to keep going. When you are low on confidence, it can be incredibly hard to imagine setting goals, but this is exactly what you should do.

Start small and write a list of four things you would like to achieve in a week. Firstly, something easily done in ten minutes, like paying a bill, returning a library book or making a phone call you have been putting off. The second goal can be a little more involved and take an hour or so – maybe batch-cooking a Bolognaise, sorting out a cupboard or going for a walk somewhere new. The third goal goes a level further and needs a longer chunk of time, like doing your tax return, meeting someone you haven't seen for ages or applying for a new job. Your fourth goal is both the easiest and hardest to do. Give yourself permission to take time out at the weekend, or on your day off, and commit to going with the flow. Ignore your lists and targets. Consider it a process for your working week and you are more likely to stick to it. There is such a feeling of accomplishment once you have a few of these goals under your belt and this can really boost your mood. Once you have settled into this pattern of steady achievement, begin to think further ahead to the future. Maybe you have been looking for a career change, considering an exciting travel opportunity or want to move somewhere new. Slowly but surely, you are taking control of your life. You are in charge.

SPIRITUAL TOOL: MANIFESTATION

If goal-setting and list-making really works for you, and you are ready to take it to the next level, look further ahead. This is the process I use, both for my professional and personal life, and would be lost without it. In my diary or a notebook, I take a page and divide it into quarters, to represent three-month chunks of time: January to March, April to June, July to September and October to December. As we lead up to each quarter, I write a list of eight goals I would like to achieve in that three-month time frame. It may be revamping my business in some way, working on a specific emotional shift with clients, a long-held dream to fly to Egypt to see the pyramids and a commitment to invest more time in a passion project. These are my manifestations to focus on. At the end of the quarter, I congratulate myself on what I have achieved, and I move any outstanding goals to a separate list. I do not automatically place them in the next quarter, because the timing or energy may not be right, so I give them space to breathe and manifest them again at a later date, relying on my intuition to know when to bring them back into focus.

Face fear with action

Three of the worst enemies of confidence are fear, rejection and failure. They are insidiously entwined, attack our self-esteem, bring havoc into our lives and can push us to make questionable decisions. It is unbelievably painful to fail or be rejected, whether it is by a family member, a friend, a lover or a potential boss, and the memory of this agony can stop us trying again. Often, we'll do anything we can to avoid facing up to the suffering, but burying our head in the sand is not a healthy solution if we want to progress, move on and make changes in our lives. We must stand firm, look the scary monsters in the eye and tell them that we will not be beaten.

At seventeen, I married my then boyfriend and by nineteen I was divorced. I had been unhappy for a while, but I didn't realise quite how much until I flew out to Tenerife to join my mum who was there on holiday. After two weeks I was dreading returning home, and I knew what I had to do. I rang my husband to tell him I wasn't coming back and that I was leaving him. It was the right decision for us both, although it was pretty awful at the time. I stayed for a month and then flew back to the UK, but my intuition was telling me to return to Tenerife. So much of my life was already up in the air, why not feel the fear and do it anyway? I sold my only possession – my Volvo – and invested the money in a friend's bar in Tenerife. My family were supportive, but I think Mum was a bit worried about me as she suggested my brother, Adam, come out with me for a while. My job, my relationship status and my home changed in an instant. It was a leap of faith, but it paid off, because I loved it there. I was so happy running the bar and I stayed for over three years.

There will be times when we fail, when we will be rejected and when we are afraid, and this, my friends, is living. Just knowing and accepting this can make it easier to deal with. The trick is to face our fears with action, because nothing dissolves it quicker than addressing it head on, having a plan and moving forward, even if it is at snail's pace. This takes courage, but believe me, we all have it in us, and the thought of failing, being spurned or trapped in the shadow of a looming fear is often more terrifying than the reality. And sometimes what we thought we wanted is not what we needed, which falls into the 'be careful what you wish for' camp.

The author and speaker Jia Jiang had a deep fear of rejection, triggered by a school event, and this defined his life for many years. As an adult who had tried his hardest to avoid being rejected, he realised he had to do something about it. He decided to run full pelt at his anxiety and embrace it, hoping he would learn from his negative experiences and transform them into the magical state of resilience. His plan was to spend 100 days actively seeking out situations where he would face rejection, to ask for things that may not be possible to be given and to take these knockbacks with upbeat positivity. Which is exactly what he did, although it didn't go quite according to plan because – spoiler alert – he found the more he was open to failure, the less it happened. It was a life-changing experience for him, to take the thing he feared the most and confront it.

I salute Jia's approach so much, and it reminds me of my mum, who taught me to see failure as positive because I could learn from it. This made me creative and brave as I grew older and is one of the reasons that I am where I am today. When I look back on my significant failures, including my education, broken friendships and money worries, I can see how much growth and truth came from each bad situation and how they all led me to this point of enlightenment. I wouldn't have it any other way.

SPIRITUAL TOOL: MEDITATION

Fill the bath with warm (not boiling hot) water and throw in three handfuls of natural sea salt. Lay back and relax. As the water begins to cool, pull the plug out and continue to lie in the bath, keeping your eyes closed. Take deep breaths of positivity and exhale negativity. Picture your anxieties draining away with the water and swirling down the plughole and into the vortex. Try not to open your eyes until all the water has gone. I often sense my spirit guide or angels close by, but you may not experience this initially or you may have a different reaction. Reflect on how you felt in the moment and write it down. Repeat the meditation the following week and see if your response to it changes. If you find this process is working for you, continue until you have had eight 'baths', monitoring your thoughts and emotions after each to see your progression.

Communication is key

As we build a positive relationship with ourselves, we need to look at how we communicate with those around us in a truthful and genuine way. These connections are key to our confidence, as is our ability to maintain a healthy balance between being with others and spending time on our own. Swinging too much in one direction can be detrimental, whether we fill our time with social demands and need to step back occasionally, or whether we find that we hide ourselves away from the world and must push ourselves outside the house once in a while.

Think hard about who you spend time with, too, and whether they are adversely affecting your self-esteem in some way. Make space for the people who fill you with happiness, who cherish the real you and encourage positivity, rather than the pessimists who drain your energy and enthusiasm. I have a strong gut instinct and can spot a Negative Nelly a mile off, so I avoid focusing on relationships that bring a complicated energy. This isn't a criticism of others; it is a realisation that we can't be friends with everyone, so we should accept this and focus on those we really connect with. That said, I am also very aware that we are all laden down with baggage invisible to the naked eye, and challenging behaviour may well be hiding serious issues, so I am mindful of this.

Being open to the changes that we need to make in our lives requires a level of honesty that we may struggle to find, both within ourselves and from those around us. To live a more authentic and free life, we have to be true to who we are and what we believe in, take responsibility for our actions, accept the consequences and live by a moral code of values. It is not our job to do this for anyone else.

Now for a slight contradiction to what I have just said. Maintaining your truth does not mean you must always share your emotional responses and anxieties with others – and where confidence is concerned, pretending to be it can be almost as good as actually being it. I highly recommend this approach if you are in a new environment and can feel your energy dipping, if something is distracting you or if you are nervous. **Inner confidence can be learned and nurtured with regular practice**. This is a good approach to use in a professional situation, as I have done in the past. I regularly give speeches and deliver presentations in front of auditoriums packed with strangers with no guarantee of how the event will go. On one occasion a man in the audience heckled me and demanded I prove my spiritual ability. I paused and then said simply, 'Your wife is standing behind you in spirit.' He shouted at me and stormed out. I didn't want to upset him, but he had asked me to show him I was not a fraud, so I did.

In the beginning, when public speaking was new to me, memories of my school days would resurface, and I would hear the spiteful voice in my head mocking my capability to get on stage. Before I went on, I would take a deep breath in and focus on my inner self, then take a long breath out and imagine the panic and anxiety leaving my body. I would repeat to myself, 'I am confident and in control and I can do this.' This was my routine before each public event and gradually I came to depend on it less and less, although I know I always have it in my toolkit should I need it.

The use of positive statements, or affirmations as they are known, can support us through a variety of difficult situations and predict a goal or state of mind before we are sure of it ourselves. I know it sounds almost too simple, but it really works. Repeating mantras on a daily basis will help to shift a negative thought pattern or rewrite a long-held belief in our subconscious, particularly where self-esteem is concerned. Words have power.

SPIRITUAL TOOL: AFFIRMATION

There are many affirmations to choose from, particularly when we talk about confidence, but there is little point repeating a positive statement you are not comfortable with, whether it is because it is too sentimental or makes you feel like you are about to get in a boxing ring. Feel free to create your own, focusing on what inspires you and what is easy to remember. I recommend starting your affirmation with the all-powerful 'I am' or 'I have'. Use the present tense, say what you want, not what you don't, and make it punchy and to the point. Do not make this about somebody else. This has to be about *you*. Here are some examples:

> 'I am confidently expressing myself openly and honestly.'
>
> 'I am powerful and in control.'
>
> 'I am strong.'
>
> 'I have the confidence to achieve whatever I set my mind to.'

Believe in yourself

Everyone is equal. This also means you. If someone behaves as if they are cleverer, funnier or more important than you, this undermines how you feel about yourself. They may not realise they are doing this, but it subdues your power and destabilises your confidence. The external voices begin to sound uncannily like your internal doubter, and you believe them because maybe, just maybe, they are right? Well, no, they are not. Do not let this happen. Listen to those you love and trust because they are the people who will support you for all the right reasons. And most importantly, believe in yourself, because you *can* be who you want to be, so hold on tightly to your dreams. **Never say, 'I can't'; always say, 'I can'.**

There are various spiritual supports you can use in this instance, such as visualisation, for example. You could imagine an invisible forcefield around you, protecting you from other people's negative feedback, and watch as their words bounce off your magnificent shield. This would also be a good time to summon your spirit guides and guardian angels, which you'll be reading more about in 'Jayne's Spiritual Kit Bag' at the end of this book.

When I was very young, I had an imaginary friend. I called her Star because she had a shiny gold star on her forehead. As I got older, she didn't disappear, and I mentioned her to my mum, who asked me to describe her and say how I felt when she was around. Star made me feel safe, protected and happy, and Mum said she was my spirit guide and was there to look after me. Star is still with me today, along with other spirit guides and guardian angels who I call upon to give me support and energy when I need it. Sometimes I feel them there when I least expect it, and this is welcome too.

In its simplest form, summoning a spirit guide or angel can be remembering a loved one who has passed away and imaging them looking over you with protection and care. You are not alone. The memory of their presence and the love they gave you is an amazingly powerful energy to channel. Let their presence reassure you. I know this won't work for everyone, but if you are curious about exploring it further, I go into more detail on page 211, including how to look for spirit signs.

For those of you who prefer the idea of an imaginary shield, there are other exercises I turn to, such as using colour as a mood enhancer. If I am feeling a little wobbly and need to boost my morale, I will often wear something red, whether it is a jumper, scarf, socks or even underwear. It makes me feel inexplicably better to see a flash of my favourite colour. As does keeping crystals close to me, which I am a big fan of, and

I write in more depth about them on page 223. Select one or several appropriate gemstones and wear them as jewellery or pop them in your pocket so you can hold them in your hand whenever you need their powerful energy.

THE ENERGY OF BLUE

Crystal: Lapis lazuli helps us focus on communication and self-awareness. A blue stone: the darker the colour, the stronger the energy.

Colour: If you do not have a crystal then find something blue to act as a talisman throughout your day, like a button or marble. Something you can keep close to you or wear.

Affirmation:

I am confident, I am strong, I am balanced.

Journal Prompt: What do I feel least confident about? How can I change this?

Step 2

LEARNING TO LISTEN TO YOUR GUT INSTINCT

Years ago, I was on holiday in Australia with my boyfriend, Lee. We were lazing by a river, enjoying the warmth and dipping into the water when we got too hot. There was a boulder in the middle of the river and Lee wanted to get a photo of me sitting on it, as a memento of our day. I am not the strongest swimmer, but I wasn't concerned as I took a leisurely breaststroke over to the rock and clambered on to pose, before swimming back to the riverbank. In the pictures Lee took, I was squinting directly into bright sunlight, so he asked me to do it again. From nowhere, I experienced a terrible sense of foreboding – a physical, stomach-clenching signal that I should not get back in the water. But why, when I had just done it?

There was no reason to worry and yet I was suddenly gripped by fear. I knew it would sound silly to voice this, so I got back in the water. I was halfway across when I could feel that something about this swim was different, as if the current had changed and I was powerless against its mighty strength. One minute my head was above water and the next I was being pulled under the surface; it all happened so fast. Lee and another guy jumped in, caught hold of me and dragged me to the bank. I was incredibly lucky and so were they. Yes, it was a big lesson in respecting and understanding open water, but it was an even bigger lesson in listening to my gut instinct. I knew something bad was going to happen and I ignored the warning.

Whether extreme or mundane, we have all been in these situations when our gut tells us something that we choose not to listen to, sometimes with catastrophic results. **Intuition is a skill we all have, but many of us find it hard to give it the attention, trust and importance it deserves** and, as practised as I am in this process, occasionally I also have to remind myself to make space for it. That sunny afternoon on an Australian riverbank is a perfect example.

Relying on our gut instinct can be deemed the weakest response to a situation, which is kind of funny when you consider that after the brain, the digestive system holds the greatest number of nerve cells. Often referred to as our 'second brain', it has over 100 million neurons, continuously sending messages around our body and linking our brain and nervous system, so there is a substantial scientific reason for trusting its reactions. It is no coincidence that we experience a physical response to moments of fear, exhilaration, uncertainty or anticipation, whether it's a feeling in the pit of our stomach, an increase in our heart rate or a sudden need to dash to the toilet. Our gut speaks to us before our head and heart wake up and smell the coffee.

Of course, our marvellous brain is our most logical tool, able to disseminate information and create a complex filing system of facts and memories which inform our decision-making, while our sensitive heart delivers overwhelming, emotional responses, based on what we want rather than what we should do. It is interesting how we often separate their responses, claiming our head has overruled our heart, or vice versa, but there are also times when both can be unreliable narrators and the most truthful reaction comes from our gut. Yet its voice is often drowned out, because while it communicates with physical symptoms, we are not always sure what their meaning is or how to act on them. If we can successfully harness all three life forces, each informing the other but allowing our intuition to lead, this should give us the answers we need.

I value my intuition above all else and have done since I was a child. My gut is my spiritual brain and my wisest self. It's the first thing I pay attention to, before my mind jumps in and attempts to take over the reins on decision-making. I try not to let anything distract me from my initial instinct so I can absorb its message, and only then listen to my emotional and logical responses. The way I describe it, it's like my gut speaks French, so my brain needs time to translate it on a Google app. This is what intuition means to me. The physical reaction I get, bad or good, reveals my truest opinion, which is then transmitted to the brain for an in-depth analysis. I think this is one of the key requirements to living a more intentional life, where we trust our physical vibrations as much as our rational and passionate thoughts. So often dismissed as spiritual clap trap, our sixth sense is as vital as the other five and an antidote to our cluttered, noisy minds. **Sometimes, listening to energy over experience gives us more clarity.**

Intuition is also the ability I rely on when I do readings for clients. The spirit messages arrive in my gut first, making my stomach churn, and I will usually feel nauseous at the beginning of a session. This sign tells me I have connected to the spirits, it is the evidence I need to continue, and I can sense a vortex of power opening up. There is a flow of energy around my body, tuning all my senses to accept this otherworldly communication and make it as easy as possible to decipher. I take a breath and wait for further confirmation. My heart may begin to ache, denoting the spirit I am communing with died from a heart attack; a twinge in my side could mean breathing issues; and a tightness in my neck indicates suicide. I pay close attention to the physical responses as well as the random thoughts, which are not my own, which pop into my head, and I share these with my client. A similar thing happens when I am healing, and the vibrations come from my gut first, before I move my hands into place.

This is how it has always happened for me. It may differ for other psychics or sound like absolute baloney to you. What can I say? I am not here to convince you to change your view, but I hope sharing this will underline how important intuition is to me in all aspects of my life. It informs who I am, and it is fundamental to my work. Of course, there are times when I sit opposite a client and I feel no physical signs of sickness or adrenalin, and I tell them. It once happened with a famous person who came in for a reading with me and I was honest and said nothing was coming through. We were both upset by this, but I recommended they return and sit down with one of my colleagues from my company, Psychic Sisters. Sometimes there is a mismatch in energy or, like the Wi-Fi, there can be a loss of signal or a faulty connection. In this instance, changing the psychic worked, the celebrity received a transformative reading and has continued to keep in touch. You can't fake or force instinct.

'Go with your gut!' we say encouragingly to each other and to ourselves when we are trying to make a decision, but without any real understanding of what this means or faith in its importance. Or we may say disappointedly, 'I wish I had listened to my gut.' We go left because our brain tells us to, but our instinct may be directing us right, and yet we decide to ignore it. Maybe because it has let us down in the past, or perhaps it is not saying what we want to hear. It is indicating a course of action that could be difficult or demanding, and nobody wants to step into an uncomfortable space, but try as we might to avoid doing hard things, this can sometimes be the way to a happier, more fulfilled life.

I once had a client, Bella, who had just suffered a ninth failed round of IVF. She wasn't sure she could put her body through a tenth cycle, but she also couldn't let go of the idea that this time it may be different. 'What does your gut say?' I asked her, and without thinking about it she said it was telling her she would be holding a boy. 'Then give it one last shot,' I said. The tenth round was successful, and Bella had twin boys. There was the possibility of a final round of IVF, and she considered it. I asked her the same question as before: 'What does your gut say?' and she answered honestly, 'It says no, don't do it.' Bella listened to it, even though she was desperate not to. 'Be blessed with what you have,' I said.

Our body is the biggest receptor we have, so tap into your own energy and decipher what it is telling you. The first step is to reconnect to our sixth sense to enable us to value and act on the big messages it sends us. There is a caveat (isn't there always), and it's this: we must remember our intuition is not always right, but, then, neither are our analytical or emotive reactions. It's just a big old game of trust, where we need to believe in ourselves and use every tool we have at our disposal to build the clearest picture possible. The more we use our intuition and are proved right, the more we trust it and make it central to our decision process.

Reframe your approach

This is a great exercise you can practise every day. When something happens, whatever it is, instead of asking others and yourself, 'What do you THINK about this?' reposition the query into 'How does this make you FEEL?' This is a subtle but vital shift to redirect power from your head to your gut and allow it to lead. It is also good to avoid a generic, 'How are you feeling?' and make it a more direct, 'How does this situation make you feel?' in order to isolate the instinct.

SPIRITUAL TOOL: JOURNALLING JOY

To be able to recognise and prioritise our gut instinct, we have to understand how we respond in a variety of situations. The quickest way to dig into this is to keep a note of your reactions and track your findings over a week. Ideally this time span should include all the small familiar moments as well as the larger, more uncomfortable happenings, so you may want to stretch it further to two or three weeks. Tune into your physical being at the beginning of each day and promise yourself you will stand as witness to what is to come. As each issue arises, whether it is someone being rude on the bus, a work problem, an argument with a family member or even procrastination over a choice of lunchtime sandwich, take a slow, controlled breath and connect to your gut. What is the feeling? Is it a stomach-clencher? A cold wave of panic? A hot fury? A mild nausea? A frisson of excitement? A heart-pounder? A tickling irritation? Have you suddenly lost your appetite or are you ravenous? Good and bad, pinpoint the physical response that comes in each individual situation and, as soon as you can, make a note of it in your book.

Now split your results into positive responses and negative ones. Our gut responds differently, pushing out anxious, stressful feelings when we are aware of being in trouble, whether this is with people or situations. How do we react to these emotions? Are we defensive? Do we push back? Or do we toe the line even when we know we shouldn't? And, faced with positive experiences, can we feel the adrenalin pumping around our system, the delicious hit of dopamine, the fluttering of excitement and the lightness of joy?

I love this exercise because it is always surprising, even for someone like me, who embraces my intuition. Firstly, it encourages you to be mindful and pay attention to the messages your body sends you. Secondly, it shows you how often and repetitive these feelings can be. Thirdly, it depicts those moments when your gut was clearly ahead of your brain. How many times did you listen to it? Star the moments when you truly let your intuition rule.

Once we have discerned these feelings, we can begin to pinpoint exactly what we are and are not comfortable with. This is how we begin to welcome our intuition. Don't dismiss any of your reactions as silly, excessive or embarrassing, because they are a true barometer of how you feel and what you want. All these physical responses are our allies, and they are lining up ready to alert us. Some of them may be awkward to sit in for too long, but do not squash them until you have acknowledged what they are and what they are trying to tell you. They are all facets of our instinct, messengers from our intuitive selves.

Taking tiny steps

With the benefit of what you have learned from your week (or two) of discovery, begin by making a few small decisions without overthinking them and getting overwhelmed. And when I say small, I mean things like getting dressed without several outfit changes, taking the lead in something minor at work or sending a text without rewriting it several times over. Replace your uncertainty and fear with a decisive attitude and be open and willing to accept the consequences that come. A bit like lining yourself up for rejection as we discussed in Step 1, you are pushing yourself out of your comfort zone and relying on your gut instinct rather than old patterns of behaviour. Welcome the uneasiness, because this means change is happening. This is about putting your intuition through its paces, not pushing it beyond its limits. There will be plenty of time for that, but for now, keep it simple and build the self-belief and trust in this new skill from within.

When I have an idea for a new product, everyone around me gives their opinion and this informs my decision-making, as it should when you are part of a team. However, if I feel very strongly about something, if just the idea of making a particular product makes me happy, then I will pursue it further. My gut tells me to do it, and I am ready to hold my hands up if it doesn't work out. I know I am lucky because I am the founder of the business, but I am still beholden to my brilliant employees and my wonderful clients, and I don't want to let any of them down. Over the years, I have honed my ability to be able to give something a go without fear of the consequences holding me back. Taking a positive approach to the unknown and opening yourself up to the possibility of failure also opens you up to the possibility of success, and things working out better than you ever imagined.

Workshop your decisions

Once you feel more confident, you can begin to make bigger changes. I am thinking of those sorts of choices where you consider moving to a different area, applying for a new job or starting or ending a relationship. These are big life decisions which I am often part of through the work I do with my clients, and I see firsthand the immobilisation that can come when we arrive at these junctions. We may well be very good at all the small stuff, but give us something weighty and life-changing and we wobble.

One of my clients, Elaine, was feeling unsettled, but could not pinpoint the root of this. Was it her job, her house, her dream of having another child, or something else entirely? She decided it was where she lived, so she sold up and bought a house on a road she had always loved. The feeling of unease didn't disappear. It nagged away at her. The problem still existed, and so she sat with it for a few months and envisioned several different lives without moving house. Elaine realised that to be able to have another child was not about having a larger house, it was about changing her career so she could be more present, and this meant a huge life change.

Not only with her job, but with the house and the area where they lived.

Firstly, don't make any rash decisions. You have been practising connecting with your intuition on a day-to-day level, so there should be a familiarity around the process, but that may not mean you are ready for the more serious stuff. Instead, imagine you have already made the decision to change whatever aspect of your life you are focusing on and visualise yourself there. Let's say you are considering moving house. Think that you will and then spend a few days workshopping how this change will look. If you can, go and shop in what might be your new local high street, do the journey from there to your work and generally immerse yourself in what this life will be. How do you feel? What is your gut telling you about this possibility? Make a few notes about your reaction to this. Now 'decide' that you are going to stay where you are and push all thoughts of moving from your mind. After a couple of days, assess how you feel about both outcomes.

This always reminds me of the scene in the American TV series *Friends*, when Rachel thinks she may be pregnant but is too scared to find out or face the truth of what this will mean. Phoebe persuades her to do a test and takes charge of reading out the result, telling Rachel it is negative. Rachel responds with exaggerated relief, but it is clear this was not the outcome she really wanted, so when Phoebe admits she lied, and that the test is positive, Rachel's reaction is truthful. Thinking that she wasn't pregnant made her realise that was exactly what she wanted to be. Her gut reaction was what counted.

I know, I am sorry to use characters in a TV show, but I can't think of a better way to illustrate my point. Sometimes the answer you think you want exposes what you truly desire. One friend always flips a coin. She chooses heads for change and tails for no change, and she pays attention to her physical reaction to the result. She says she always knows what she wants this way, because if it lands heads and her immediate response is disappointment or to change the rules to the best of three, then she knows it's tails for her. Alternatively, you could try my Pros and Cons exercise, below.

SPIRITUAL TOOL: PROS AND CONS

This is a good way to help solve a dilemma you may be faced with. Let's take the idea of changing your job as an example. You have the opportunity to leave for new horizons, but you are unsure whether the move is advisable. Take a clean sheet of paper and head it 'Should I Stay in My Job?', then draw a line down the middle of the paper, creating two columns, the subheading 'Stay' on the left and 'Go' on the right. On the left, write a positive reason why you should stay in your current job. Let's say it is because the team you work with are great. In the 'Go' column, counteract this with what you could gain from leaving, which could be a new group of friendships and contacts. Now move on to the next point. Maybe the money is good where you are now, but if you go, there are better promotional prospects in the new role. Continue with as many substantial points as you need to list, but try to focus on key issues and keep your list to ten points so that you're not overwhelmed.

Now you need to grade each point out of eight. How crucial is it to you to have good relationships with your colleagues? Mark it on a scale of one (not important at all) to eight (absolutely crucial). Does the idea of meeting new people and expanding your professional network appeal? Maybe it's an average four, or a strong seven. You get the idea. Go through the list until you have a number next to each point, then add up the first column and write the total at the bottom before doing the same with the second. You should find one outweighs the other, giving you a winner and an indication of your final decision. Conversely, if you are disappointed by this result and wish the other column had won, then there is your answer.

No sudden moves

We all need to be reminded of this. When we want to change things, we become impatient, quieten our intuition and push to an answer that may not be the right one. Take your time.

If you are awash with complicated feelings or are behaving like a rabbit caught in the headlights, take a short breather and give your brain a break. Do something unconnected to the decision you are trying to make. If you can, immerse yourself in nature with a walk in the woods or along the beach, and if you can't, go and sit in the garden or on your doorstep with a cup of tea, bake a cake, or spend an evening focused on a hobby. It can also be therapeutic to do the laundry and achieve something tangible, even if it is a pile of neatly folded clothes. Our intuition can be easily scared off, so treat it gently, like cupping a butterfly in your hands, and allow it to resurface. You will hear it better in a quiet, calm space.

Do and don't care what people think

One of the ways to measure how you truly feel about something is to share your thoughts with those close to you, someone you can trust. Tell them your dilemma, welcome their opinion and monitor how this makes you feel. Do you have a surge of energy, knowing what they have said is right, or has their view cemented the reverse in your mind? This is where the 'not caring what people think' bit comes in, because you may be just as likely to disagree with them as agree and, if it is the former, then pay heed to this. Do not make a decision based on what they say; let the conversation stimulate your intuition and lead you to your own conclusions.

Sit in the uncomfortable

This is a crucial part of the process in understanding and acting on our gut instinct. There are times when our gut tells us something which our head and heart will then persuade us to ignore. Occasionally I will have an intuitive response to something or someone, but I am too busy to take notice of what it is telling me, so my brain disconnects from the messages it is bombarded with, overrides my intuition and powers me through the rest of the day. And yet, while I am lulled into a false sense of being okay, I have a nagging sense of something hanging over me. My intuition will nudge me regularly until I have addressed the issue.

It can be incredibly difficult to face the hard things our intuition may be telling us. It reminds me of a friend of mine, Sharon, who went to Paris with her long-term boyfriend and, when they were at the top of the Eiffel Tower, he proposed. Before that moment she would have said that was exactly what she wanted to happen. After all, they had been together for years, they had a flat and, other than the usual disagreements, there was no indication they would split up. When he went down on one knee, several things happened to her. First, her gut said 'No'. Then her heart said, 'But I don't want to break up with him because that will hurt' and her brain said, 'Plus you have a mortgage together.' So, Sharon said yes. The truth was that neither of them really wanted to get married. They both knew it wasn't right, but they couldn't face what the truth meant until a few months later, when her boyfriend left her for someone else, saving himself and Sharon from a terrible mistake. This is a big lesson in not making the wrong choice just because the right choice is too painful to contemplate.

None of us wants to be uncomfortable, it's not a good feeling, but if our intuition is leading us there, it may have a point. It could be showing us that sometimes we have to face hard facts in order to move forward. Do not supress it; instead, welcome it with open arms and take the time to understand what it is telling you. Of course, it could turn out to be wrong, so, as I have already mentioned, do not make any kneejerk decisions: just be aware that it is there and pointing in a direction you may need to go.

SPIRITUAL TOOL: ASKING FOR SIGNS

Looking for a sign is a helpful tool in supporting our intuition. We may not have the confidence to trust our gut entirely, but if we throw the question out to the universe too, then it will answer. I do this in a number of ways, maybe with an angel message of affirmation, whether this is seeing a number I have already chosen, finding a white feather, or asking for a sign in the form of something – usually a robin, but you can pick anything that pops into your head. (I go into this in more detail on page 216.) I will also use a particular song as a support.

> For example, when my team and I are in the middle of a stressful work week, we will often sing 'Just Keep Swimming' from the film *Finding Nemo*.
>
> Tapping into our senses helps to ground us and give us time to recalibrate. In particular, scents are powerful triggers to transport us to safe spaces. Whether it is a nostalgic smell from our childhood, a favourite flower or a healing herb like sage, spritzing yourself or the air around you can help you relax and focus.

You won't always get it right

A few years ago, I was approached by a client who was keen to partner with me on a wellness brand. We spent time working together on an idea, but I had a nagging doubt about their motivation behind this, even though there was no reason to question them. I didn't listen to my gut, and instead I listened to what the client and their team were telling me. I hoped they were genuine, and yet when they fed off my energy, took my ideas and created something for themselves without any reference to where their inspiration had come from, I was unsurprised. When it happened, I knew this would be the outcome, but I had not let myself believe it. So, you see, I can still get caught out. My gut told me not to go ahead, but I chose to take the risk and it didn't pay off. Sometimes we have to do this. The trick is not to silence our intuitive voice, but to turn to it throughout the experience, monitor those gut responses and be ready to take action. That was another big lesson to learn.

Do not be put off by those times you listened to your gut and got it wrong, because this can just as likely happen as ignoring it and making a mistake. Sometimes we manipulate our instinct because we know what we want and we are going to do it regardless. There is no such thing as not having intuition or being 'bad at it'; it is about how easily you are able to access and interpret gut instinct and incorporate your logical and emotional reactions too.

There are situations when you have to ignore your gut instinct. It can be misleading, or struggling with a past issue that informs a present experience. Like having a car accident and then being convinced it will be repeated if you get back behind the wheel. This isn't intuition; this is fear.

I want to share a very personal memory at this point. Many years ago, my dad, who had been poorly for some time, was in a lot of pain and couldn't get out of bed. He had returned home after difficult prostate surgery, and he didn't want to go back into hospital. He was scared that if he did, he wouldn't come home again. He told me not to call the ambulance, but I couldn't stand to see him suffering. I ignored what he told me and rang the emergency number. My instinct was that he was near the end of his life, but I was still prepared to do whatever it took to keep him in this world as long as possible. I could feel my spirit guide, the presence of my mum, telling me to let him go, but my head and heart overruled her because they had to. I think we would all respond like this. As clear as both my instruction from him and my intuition were, I didn't listen to either because in this situation they had to be ignored. Once in hospital, it was clear Dad had very little time left and I stayed by his side until the end. I felt my mum come to collect him. I did question whether I had made the right decision, but I am glad I trusted my gut.

SPIRITUAL TOOL: CHAKRA

Chakras are energy points throughout our body, the most significant of which are the seven running in a line from the top of our head to the base of our spine (you can read more about chakras in the final chapter, 'Jayne's Spiritual Kit Bag', page 219). Usually we work through the central chakras, starting at the crown of the head, moving to the third eye in the middle of the forehead, followed by the throat, heart, solar plexus, sacral and root, but I believe that while guidelines are useful at the beginning of your journey to enlightenment, you can start wherever you wish, or focus on one chakra at a time. I often start a healing mediation with the solar plexus, the fifth chakra, focusing on my gut and clearing and cleansing before I move on to others. I listen to the vibrations in my body and let my intuition lead me to my chakras in whatever order it thinks, maybe to my heart for emotional issues or the third eye for focus.

Sit in quiet place. (I say this, but I often do this meditation on the train, so wherever you feel able to concentrate for a few minutes.) Eyes open or closed, breathe in healing energy through your mouth, take it all the way down to your solar plexus and imagine pushing the energy out to whichever chakra you intuitively think needs it most before you breathe out. As you exhale, send the energy out to the universe. While you do this you can place your hand on your navel and connect with your solar plexus chakra. See it as yellow – its defining colour – and visualise breathing the colour in and pushing the energy out.

Take the plunge

You are ready. Begin your intuitive future right now. Be honest with yourself and practise and gain confidence in trusting your reactions. This will light the way for where you step next.

I often find it useful to write down how I am feeling and the current issue I may be faced with. Give the page a heading, like 'I am not sure I want to maintain a friendship with Susan', then write three subheadings: Gut, Brain, Heart. Now note what each of these is telling you about your relationship. For example, under 'Gut' you may say that you no longer feel that you and Susan have much in common and you don't enjoy her company. Under 'Brain', you write that you have known Susan a long time and she has been there for you through tough times. Under 'Heart', you may note that you do not want to hurt her feelings and what happens if you make a mistake and miss her? Now continue to write down your thoughts around this. You may find that as you commit it all to paper, you reach a deeper understanding of a complicated dilemma. You may not always get a clear answer, but noting your thought process and seeing what really matters will help. As you come to the end of the practice, consider what you want the result to be and manifest it by jotting this down too. Combining manifestation and your faith in knowing what is right for you is a powerful duo.

THE ENERGY OF YELLOW

Crystal: Citrine is the crystal for this chapter. It is yellow, representing the colour of the solar plexus, and it is tasked with guiding us towards better intuition, helping our digestion, manifesting abundance, free will and finding balance. When you meditate, place the crystal in your lap or on your tummy above your navel.

Colour: Whether you have a crystal or not, bringing more yellows into your life is a good thing. Why not make your first drink of the day a hot water with lemon, which is a great digestive detox and starts the morning on the right note? Carry around something yellow as a talisman to connect to your intuition or wear a yellow item of clothing. You could even spritz yourself with a fresh lemon scent. All of these ideas are helpful tools to encourage intuition.

Affirmation:

I listen to my inner voice to guide me.

Journal Prompt: What is my inner voice saying to me about work, relationships, home life and dreams? How can I make space for it in my everyday?

Step 3

FINDING AND SETTING BOUNDARIES

When I was twelve, I was rushed to hospital with a serious hip issue that kept me in traction for a month and then bedbound with rheumatoid arthritis. Up until this point, I had been super sporty and ran for the county, but suddenly my whole young world came crashing down around me. I had to take a year off school, and when I returned, everything had changed because of my disability. I was severely bullied, called a cripple, and comments were also made about my lovely mum because she used crutches after having polio as a child.

As the daily target of playground tormenters, I believed what they said about me and allowed them to undermine my self-confidence. I made myself as small and insignificant as possible in the hope I would be invisible to them, but it didn't work. At fourteen I left school, battered and broken by the experience combined with the difficulties of my illness. Where were the guardian angels I had wholeheartedly believed in? I was incensed that they had let me down. Surely it was

FINDING AND SETTING BOUNDARIES

their job to warn me about such a life-changing situation. Overnight, I shut them down, even though this was exactly the moment when I needed their support. I switched off the channel of communication between us and I stopped believing for several years.

I took a different path through the remainder of my education and gradually my attitude to myself and my ability began to shift, partly helped by the seven siblings I grew up with – we are a big family of eight kids! At home, I had to shout to be heard, and this reawakened the person I was before the bullies and hospital stay, and I went from a quiet, shy wallflower to a mouthy dynamo who could stand up for herself. As my voice, opinion and strength re-emerged from its enforced hibernation, I began to draw lines to protect these hard-won skills. Without realising it, I was building the boundaries which have continued to support me throughout my life, albeit with occasional diversions and mistakes along the way.

Recognising, constructing and holding respectful boundaries is a thoroughly modern dilemma which carries a whiff of negativity among those who dismiss it as 'therapy speak'. Healthy boundaries rely on good connections with gut instinct to understand our feelings and desires and to place them at the centre of our lives. It is not about being selfish, demanding, dismissive or rude, but this is how it might come across to those who would prefer us to stay exactly as we are. **Remember, it is not about them and what they want from you; this is about what you want from yourself**. It is a difficult process and demands a level of honesty we may not have connected with before, but it is also an integral part of creating a happy intentional life. This is where we find our real meaning, our deepest thoughts, our most truthful self.

We are creating a place of safety, not just for ourselves but for those around us, and this is thrown into sharp relief when we have children. I am not a parent, but I have friends and family who have navigated the anxiety-ridden crash course of boundary-setting with their kids. This is the version where we create borders for someone we unconditionally love who will relentlessly and often angrily push against them, causing us to continually question our decisions. Without judgement, but with experience, I say a child lacking boundaries will feel unsafe, unhappy and scared, just as we do as adults. Giving people a structure and an understanding of what is required from them can instil a deep mutual trust.

There are also the boundaries we struggle with around the addictive parts of our personalities, whether we struggle with our relationship to cigarettes, alcohol, drugs, food, exercise or work. While this chapter focuses on our relationships with others, there are spiritual tips that may help with any wider areas where you'd like to see change in your life.

The good news is that once you have a structure in place, it is much easier to maintain than you may think, and it is also in your power to reshape whenever you are ready. I learned this through establishing my boundaries as a teenager and testing, stretching and reforming them in the years that followed. We set the standard for what is acceptable, but we often forget it is in our power to do so. **Boundaries are a form of respect which others can show us and which we can show ourselves.**

The trick is to know when to hold on tightly to them and when you can loosen your grip.

So, what are personal boundaries?

They are the self-governed limits we place on ourselves and the relationships around us, which empower us to make decisions, protect our mental wellbeing and nurture self-respect. I like to think of them as mindful borders, the edges between us and the person we are with or the situation we are in, that we set to shield as well as promote our authentic core. Drawing these invisible lines and communicating them to others can be a fraught process, but imagine if you could create a powerful blueprint which enables you to live your best life. Just writing that makes it feel as if the sun has suddenly come out from behind a dark cloud.

Fire up the gut instinct

To understand which boundaries need to be put in place, we have to encourage our intuitive self to speak up. We talked about connecting with our gut instinct in the previous chapter, so here is a perfect opportunity to put it into practice. Give yourself an appraisal period of at least a week and, as you go about your day, at home, at work, with loved ones and friends, be attuned to how your gut is responding and jot down the results. You may already know the areas where you need to instil stronger boundaries, but this exercise is worth doing because there is often a deep-seated historic issue you will have subconsciously ignored or something that surprises you. Let's look at what may come up.

Do you struggle with...

- **Emotional boundaries?** Maybe with the way your partner responds to your needs, perhaps your parents continue to treat you as a child, or you are a people-pleaser who is afraid of being rejected?

- **Physical boundaries?** Which can translate to both the space around you – home, office, gym – and your bodily self – people's overfamiliarity, sexual activity. How often have you wanted to keep someone at actual arm's length or to be alone in a room?

- **Practical boundaries?** These could include lending people things you would prefer not to, like treasured possessions or money you have worked hard to earn. What may have been once or twice can quickly turn into someone taking advantage of your generosity with an expectation this will continue. This also includes your precious time. How regularly do you say yes to things you do not want to go to or spend time with someone when you wish you hadn't?

- **Unhealthy boundaries?** Maybe you are too rigid with some rules and incredibly lax on other things. Or repeatedly attempt to set boundaries only to watch them be knocked down by those you are close to. Do you recognise which of your boundaries are healthy and which could be creating a toxic situation for you? Is there an addiction you struggle with around alcohol, drugs, food or exercise?

- **Other people's boundaries?** Do you feel manipulated by boundaries that are not yours or that these are more worthy than your own? Perhaps you latch on to others' boundaries because you do not have the confidence to instil your own.

To work out what you may want to focus on, take your cue from your physical response to people and situations and consider what the issue is around it. Don't listen to your inner voice saying you can't face an issue or allow it to dictate what your boundaries should be, because this kneejerk reaction comes from a place of fear, not enlightenment. I think we all have work to do in at least one of these areas. I know I do.

In my past I was attracted to people who needed more from me than I ever should have given. Maybe this stems from being lonely at school and believing that any friends were better than no friends, but I forged relationships which I subconsciously knew were bad for me. I put others' needs and demands before my own, for fear of losing people, and I would go out of my way to help, which didn't always work out, emotionally and financially – if someone asked to borrow money, I was likely to lend it to them. While I have never forgotten my dad's advice to not trust people until they have proved themselves, I am also a product of a family who had very little but would help others if we could.

I can still be a sucker for a sob story if I believe it is coming from a place of truth and vulnerability and I may relax my boundaries in these situations. It is in my nature to help, and I try to give people the benefit of the doubt unless my intuition tells me otherwise. It has only been in the last few years that I have managed to build and maintain a boundary around this issue. I am incredibly careful, but the truth is I would prefer to risk those rare occasions when my trust is broken rather than question everyone's motives because that is who I am. I am prepared to let my barrier down for someone who is really struggling for whatever reason if I genuinely feel I can help. That said, once I feel the energy change and realise someone is being insincere or taking advantage of me, my shutters come down instantly.

SPIRITUAL TOOL: THE THREE CIRCLES

Here is a great exercise to help you work out whether you need a boundary on a particular issue. Take an A4 piece of paper and write at the top of the page the question you are asking. Let's say you are uncomfortable with a friendship and want to know if you should step back. Now draw a circle the size of a tennis ball in the middle. Leaving a good border to allow you to write in, draw a second circle outside the first. Repeat again so you have three circles. In the middle circle write all the good things about continuing with the relationship. In the next ring write any points you are unsure about and in the outer ring note the issues you have a real problem with. In the first instance, this clearly sets out the good, questionable and bad points for you to consider and which section is the fullest. Secondly, close your eyes, hover your pen over the paper and think about the question before dropping the pen. Where does it land? If in the middle, then how does this make you feel? Are there enough positives which encourage you to maintain the friendship? If it lands in the outer circle, do you think you can establish a boundary?

Take your time

Don't rush to construct all your boundaries at once. This is a careful process that takes time and is likely to involve family, friends and work colleagues who are unaware of the ground rules you want to put in place, so resist dramatically pulling up the drawbridge. Some of the boundaries you want to create might be hard, for those around you and for yourself, so don't pile on the pressure and just begin with small but significant changes. Too much too quickly could result in a crash of faith and energy further down the line.

You may want to start by tackling an issue that is not connected to a person but instead could be a habit that you are trying to break. Choose a boundary you would like to work on and set yourself a couple of goals connected to it. For example, if you are trying to give up smoking, begin by cutting down on the number of cigarettes you smoke in a day. This is an obvious one, but gaining strength from this achievement will help boost your confidence and encourage you to keep going. Alternatively, if you feel there are co-dependency issues, maybe with a parent or friend, then make a gentle move, perhaps by not calling them back immediately or saying you can't come over that day. Whatever you want to explore, be proud of what you are accomplishing and **do not be tempted or persuaded to relinquish control of your fledgling boundaries – you are setting them for a reason.**

SPIRITUAL TOOL: VISUALISATION FOR LETTING GO OF NEGATIVE THOUGHTS

Imagine you are a ranch hand, sitting astride a wild and beautiful horse. You are holding a thick rope in your hand. Throw it out in front of you and lasso an unwelcome thought, pull the rope tightly and drag it to a pen to trap it. Shut the gate, draw the heavy bolt across, tip your Stetson to the bad thought then tap your heel into your trusty steed and trot away, leaving the thought behind you.

Firm but fair

Once we have an understanding of which boundaries are important to us, we need to consider how we are going to share this message to those who need to hear it. It would be unfair on loved ones to construct boundaries that impact them without explaining what we are doing. It is also important to say how we feel in a clear and calm manner, so it might help to make some notes to help organise your thoughts and refer to during the conversation. Choose a good time to broach the subject and adopt a firm but kind approach, being aware of the language you are using. You may decide to take the personal sting out of a situation by talking about it in a broader sense, but this can also bring its own problems if the message is misconstrued or lost, so be direct and try not to waffle. Don't be surprised if the person you are speaking to has their own boundary issue they want to discuss – if so, allow it space. This is not a game of 'Rock, Paper, Scissors' where one of you trumps the other. Instead, see this as an opportunity for you both to discuss how you feel and to find a compromise from a place of mutual respect.

Having shared my weakest boundary, let me tell you about one of my strongest, which is to ensure that I protect my time. I have learned to always be able to communicate this clearly. If a friend invites me somewhere, like a restaurant, to see a play or go on a trip, that I don't want to go to, I say, 'No, thanks.' I don't make up excuses or pretend I would have loved to have gone but I'm unavailable. The decision not to go could come from having done too much already this week or having been busy at work, and I may use that as a reason, but equally if I just don't fancy it, I will say that. I maintain that you don't need to give an excuse, but if you feel that you have to, one is enough, and any more than that can begin to sound fake. I imagine this sounds rude to those not used to this approach, and I certainly don't want to hurt anyone's feelings, but my small bubble of friends and family know that this is how I deal with things, and they respect my honesty. They know I won't go somewhere out of a sense of duty or guilt and because of this, they know where they stand with me. If someone asks a favour, I don't feel obliged to do it – I do it because I want to and I use my intuition to steer me towards those who really need my help and away from those who don't.

Being truthful has given me stronger, happier relationships and has cleared space for those who benefit from it, including myself. Many years ago, I learned the vital lesson that time is one of our most valuable commodities and I decided not to squander it. The best way to work out relationship boundaries is to measure the amount of time something will take against whether that is your best use of it. If you decide to give your time as a gift to somebody else, then do so wholeheartedly, but if you feel a niggling resentment that may be telling you that this really isn't how you want to spend your evening or your day off, then **you are perfectly entitled to say, 'No, thanks.'** There may also be something you really don't want to do but it's very hard to get out of and you feel guilty about it. Equally, you shouldn't feel obliged to go against your boundaries and go along with something that you're not comfortable with. I had this recently when a friend asked me to go to his mother's funeral. I find funerals really difficult for lots of different reasons, so I took the time to explain to him how I felt, and offered other practical and emotional ways to support him. In turn, he understood my feelings and relied on me in other ways. By being honest, I could support him without compromising my own wellbeing.

Put your own oxygen mask on first

With every boundary you put in place there is likely to be a mixed reaction from those around you. This is probably why you haven't done this before now. We all care about what other people think and we do not want to hurt anyone in our mission to make our lives happier. Putting ourselves first is much harder than we realise, and it is often seen as a self-centred act, but what if it was a case of survival? Compare it to watching the safety briefing on an aeroplane and being told to put your own oxygen mask on first before you can begin to help others. We can only take responsibility for our own actions and emotions and be true to how we feel. **By reclaiming ourselves, we are not abandoning others**, even if their response is to push against our boundary, believing it to be weak in the face of what they need. This is really them saying that we are invisible, and it is their needs that matter more, not ours.

Understanding that we might sometimes create co-dependent habits can make boundary-building more complicated. I had a client who had been supporting a friend through a bad marriage break-up. Let's call them Nicki and Kate. Nicki spent a lot of time with Kate, helping her through legal issues, emotional breakdowns and practical problems. Every conversation revolved around the divorce and Kate's needs, but this made Nicki feel closer to her and like she was fulfilling the role of a good friend. This was important to Nicki. Gradually Kate moved on, got a new boyfriend and was happy, but somewhere amongst it all she forgot that Nicki existed outside of the drama. Every time they met, Kate would continue to talk about herself and forget to ask Nicki about what was going on in her life. Nicki began to resent this and instead of speaking out about how she felt, she decided to pull back and spend her time with friends she had a more balanced relationship with. It took a while for Kate to realise this, but when she did, she accused Nicki of abandoning her.

Nicki gained strength through the readings with me, and we discussed her issue. She chose to be honest with Kate about her reasons for doing so, saying that she felt the friendship had become one-sided and that some time apart would help them both reevaluate what they wanted from it. This was a brave step for Nicki, who was still learning how to put herself first and understanding how she encouraged co-dependent behaviour. Kate listened, apologised and promised to make more effort in future. Of course, there aren't always happy endings, but this story shows how easily we can become trapped in patterns of behaviour, both our own and with others, and demonstrates that we do have the power to change it if we just speak out. Kate had no idea how Nicki felt, and once she did, she wanted to do something about it. Nicki could have voiced this earlier. This wasn't about apportioning blame; it was about recognising the negative direction the friendship had gone in and both taking responsibility for changing it. Well done, Nicki and Kate!

SPIRITUAL TOOL: BUBBLE UP

This is an exercise I rely on when I feel my boundaries are being questioned by someone, whether that is emotionally or physically. One of the best times to use it is when you are in a crowded public place, an open-plan office or somewhere impossible to escape from other people. I often use it when I am squashed on an underground train and facing a stranger's armpit. In your head, say, 'Bubble up!' and imagine being immediately encased in a safe, protective bubble separate from whatever is going on around you. Now visualise a place where you love to be without closing your eyes. It could be your back garden, a favourite holiday beach destination or your own bedroom. I take myself to the fields near my house. Once you have chosen your safe haven, then this is your default place to go, a bit like a screensaver. You can't pick multiple destinations; it needs to be the same place every time, so you can easily summon it and instantly it

> will transport you. Don't waste time trying to remember the detail of somewhere special, just go to the place that gives you the feeling of security. Aim to stay in the bubble for a few minutes, longer if you need to, and then repeat the command, this time saying, 'Bubble down!'

Nobody said it would be easy

While none of us want to spend time in an awkward or uncomfortable situation, this is where the real work begins and demonstrates how committed we are to making changes. My friend Lucy was a terrible people-pleaser who was confident and in control at work but found it hard to assert herself or put her needs first in her personal life. Over the years this meant she wasted time in relationships that were not right for her, she did what others expected of her and sometimes she couldn't even decide what to order in a restaurant until everyone else had. On the one hand she was a professional career person and on the other she was the emotional dependent, which was confusing for her and surprising to others.

After a particularly bad period in her life, when she combined business with friendship and set up a company with two pals which then imploded, she realised enough was enough. She sat in the awfulness of the situation. As desperate as she was to rush the process, she stopped and waited for her intuitive voice to surface and, when it did, it was loud and clear. This is where she began to take control of her life. She worked hard to understand herself better, where her need to please came from and what it would take to build boundaries she had never had. It was slow-going but she continued moving forwards, questioning relationships, decisions and desires. Now she is where she wants to be, with fewer friends but able to spend more time with the ones she chooses to. She says no to things she doesn't want to do. She looks at a menu and chooses what she instinctively wants to eat. Every time she senses the familiar wobble of morphing into the person someone else wants, she takes a moment, a few deep breaths and asks herself, 'What do YOU want?'

SPIRITUAL TOOL: PENDULUM

This is one of my favourite exercises because it harnesses our spiritual self with ease and shares insightful results through the ancient art of divination – a physical practice used to predict the future. You do not need an actual pendulum for this; it works just as well with a ring or a crystal as the weight on the end of a string. It responds to psychic vibrations from both within us and our spirit guides, giving answers to our burning questions through movement; back and forth, in a circle, or erratic.

Think of a question you would like to ask, which can be as big or as small as you want, but it must elicit a 'yes' or 'no' answer. Make sure you are somewhere quiet with your 'pendulum' in your hand and take a few deep breaths, or a moment of meditation before you begin, because any heightened feelings could affect the reading. Now, tell the pendulum how you will read its movements. You can even do a run-through with a few basic questions. There are no hard-and-fast rules about deciphering the pendulum; you can set your own or use mine, which is back and forth for 'yes' and in a circle for 'no'. If it can't make up its mind, I call this haywire and take it as a maybe or that confusion around the issue is too heavy to cut through. If this is the answer you get, then stop and come back to it again in a few days.

When you are ready, the best place to sit is at a table so you can rest your elbow on the surface and let the pendulum hang from one hand. Hold it purposefully, but without tension, and allow it and your mind to settle. Ask your question and wait for the pendulum to begin to move gently. If this is the first time you have tried this spiritual practice, you may not get a clear response, but do not give up. Take a break and come back to it again later. If you have several questions to ask, I recommend starting with the biggest one, e.g. 'Should I sell my house?', and then ask the smaller, more detailed ones around this statement, e.g. 'Should I move area?'

∞

Testing boundaries

As you put your structure in place and are open about your needs, it is inevitable that there will be people who will not respect this. They may not do so consciously, but they will persuasively push against the barrier you have set up or dismissively hurdle it, in an attempt to put things back to how they were and make themselves feel better. Perhaps this is because they struggle with establishing their own boundaries, have toxic or abusive tendencies, exist in repetitive behavioural patterns they are unaware of, or they just don't understand what you are doing. Whatever it is they are dealing with, it is their issue, not yours. Their response doesn't mean your boundary no longer exists or was worthless; it means you need to repeat what it is and make your expectations around it clear. Don't be angry or frustrated, because this is part of establishing a longer-term understanding and it is normal for new boundaries to be tested and questioned initially.

If their behaviour destabilises you, take some time to think about how to respond. You don't need to jump into this immediately – take time out to consider your feelings and look into yourself. Sometimes we all need a breather before we can respond with sincerity and clarity and anything less than this is a disservice to you and the other person. I continue to check my boundaries, like locking up the house at night and making sure the windows are shut and the front door is secure. I ask myself what I think about something, do I really want to do whatever I am asked to do, am I happy with the way someone has behaved, and I interrogate my responses.

I do this with my spiritual boundaries too. If I am doing a reading and I don't like the energy of the spirit who is coming through, I tell them to leave and I shut down the channel to disable them.

Back in this world, if your boundaries are being ignored, then you may need to set a consequence in place to reiterate how you feel, and stick to it. Any vagueness around your boundaries will create chinks, which will turn into holes large enough for several people to climb through. It may be that you need to take a break from the person involved and the seriousness of this action will help underline the point you are making. **Don't throw empty threats around. If you set the rules, then you need to stick to them**. When I worked on my boundary around the emotional and financial bolstering I was doing for unsuitable friendships, there were a few changes I could make quickly. Like calming my usually buzzy energy, which I know attracts people to me and means they see me as a doer, a solver and a safe pair of hands. By containing this vibrancy, I was less attractive to them. I did something even more important: I stopped getting my credit card out and paying for lunch. The people closest to me now are what I call my '2am Gang' – the friends I could ring in the middle of the night if I needed them and they would be there for me. Surround yourself with the people who have got your back, who bring emotional rewards and those who can pick you up and put you back on track when you need it.

A word here on flexibility, which may feel a little like it contradicts what I have just said, but it's important to also remember that a boundary is not a solid, immovable barrier.

It will change and adapt as our priorities shift, relationships develop, and we gain a better understanding of who we are. We will have different boundaries depending on who we are with, so we can relax or fortify accordingly. The point is that **our boundaries are under our control**.

This reminds me of Cath, a client who moved to a new area where she knew nobody and was keen to make friends. The quickest way to do this was at the school gate when she picked up her child, and so she set about ingratiating herself to everyone she met. With very little time and trouble, Cath had amassed a large group of acquaintances which she then spent a couple of years pandering to, feeding these relationships like a large beast who was constantly hungry. She had created a monster. In the midst of it all, she was unhappy, unfulfilled, tired and, ironically, lonely. She took two courses of action, setting instant boundaries with those people she did not want to continue to get to know and then took a more gradual approach with the people she liked, where she set softer boundaries to help build a deeper connection. Cath stopped going to every social event she was invited to and she scaled back on the number of times she had people over to her house. Ultimately, she forged several strong friendships and the friendships that were not meant to be fell by the wayside.

I think of my positive friendships as streams which run through my life, consistent, present and yet ever ebbing and flowing. I have a relatively new friend who does not ask anything of me. I am hoping she becomes a stream in my life. I don't need her, but I would like her to stay around, and I would miss her if she disappeared. We are building our relationship based on the robust boundaries that we are both very open about and I can see how this will stand us in good stead for the future.

> **SPIRITUAL TOOL: MEDITATION FOR BOUNDARIES**
>
> Find a quiet, private place to sit comfortably. Close your eyes and take a long, deep breath in through your nose, hold it for a few seconds and then exhale through your mouth. Repeat this several times and as you do so, begin to think about a moment when your boundaries were compromised, either by yourself or someone else. How did this make you feel? Sit with the emotion that comes from this. Were you angry, frustrated, upset, disappointed? Now, think about how you could have dealt with the situation in a different way. Walk yourself through this scenario, imagining how different the outcome might have been. Do not apportion any blame. With your next breath in, reset your mind and tell yourself you are able to set meaningful boundaries, and as you breathe out, let the annoyance and stress go.

Blurring boundaries

The blurring of boundaries is incredibly common in all areas of our lives, particularly within family dynamics and work situations, and can take a significant redrawing of goal posts. Coming from a big family, I had a lot of practice of holding my own needs in the face of emotional pushing and shoving from those around me, and I continue to experience this in my professional life too. In the past, there have been clients who have called me any time of the day or night for a reading, and I haven't turned them away. Now, only my friends have my mobile phone number, which gives me the space I need and gently tells my clients that I am not prepared to always be available to them.

As a psychic, I am regularly asked to do readings when I am not working. If someone knows what I do, they may ask me a leading question or start talking about the state of their relationship and whether I have any sense of where it may be heading. They may even ask if I have a message for them from their dead auntie. This is the same as having dinner with a doctor friend and suddenly rolling up your trouser leg to show them a large lump on your calf. I am very good at deflecting this sort of behaviour and do it all the time. It also means that when I choose to give someone a reading, it is because I want to, and it is my decision to do it. Recently I was in a TV studio, and I was chatting to the presenter off camera. I knew something wasn't right and she told me her mother had died recently and she was finding everything tough. I had my tarot cards with me and offered her a reading. She began to refuse, saying that was not what she had been angling for, and I knew that. The very fact that she hadn't been asking me had made me want to help.

A similar thing happened with a freelance professional, John, who was working with me on a project. He was uncomfortable around the idea of the spirit world and open about his scepticism. He didn't ask me to prove anything, and I didn't feel like I needed to, but I got a message from his mum which I passed on to him. John was sure that the information I had was incorrect and I shrugged, saying I didn't always get it right. That evening he spoke to his dad and the following day he called me to apologise as his dad had corroborated what I had said. I also gave him the final message from his mum, which was to find her ring and give it to his wife to wear. She told me it was in a box with John's watch and, sure enough, that was where he found it.

Respecting boundaries

Just as you ask others to respect your boundaries, so you must do the same for them. They may not be able to set and state their restrictions as clearly as you can. Or they do, but you have misinterpreted or chosen to ignore them. I think we have all been guilty of this and it is often in asserting our own boundaries that it teaches us to understand and respect other people's. If I overstep the mark and I'm pulled up on it, it may feel hurtful, but I am getting better at managing my emotions and not letting them slip into stubbornness. It helps knowing that the other person has battled to set their boundary and it really matters to them even if it seems excessive or pointless to others. **It is not for us to judge whether someone else's boundary is 'right' or 'wrong'**; it is only for us to know whether we can accept their desires, offer a compromise if not, or step back entirely. If we can embrace the combination of balance, acceptance and mutual respect, then this can only lead to better, happier relationships with others and ourselves.

Practical boundaries

This is a complex part of boundary-building and, while I do not want this to feel like a footnote in the chapter, this is not the place, and I am not the person to deep-dive into this. I am talking about the boundaries around addiction. When I was a kid, the TV programme *Grange Hill* covered an important storyline around substance addiction and released a single, 'Just Say No', to warn of the dangers of drug-taking. The premise was that if you were offered something, you should just say no and not succumb to peer pressure, yet it didn't address how damn hard it is to say no to yourself.

It is easy to relate this to drugs and alcohol, but what about boundaries with other things that are much harder to avoid, like food? Or our reliance on technical gadgets, specifically mobile phones? In some instances, it is possible for us to put constraints in place with our addictions and boost our willpower to support these decisions. For example, setting rules around your mobile phone usage by leaving it in another room, downloading restrictions on the handset, not having it out on the dinner table or taking it to bed with you is a great start. Implementing change in other destructive behaviours is much harder, and I would be a fool to suggest small steps work for serious addictions. What is important is recognising the concrete boundaries you have enforced to protect and sustain your addictions and understanding that the help you will need exists beyond this book.

There have been times when my work has been a catalyst for people to seek help. Many years ago, a woman, Lizzie, came in for a reading. She looked smart and sophisticated, was charming and articulate, and when she sat down in front of me, she seemed almost perfect – and yet I felt uncomfortable. Her mum came through from spirit and told me Lizzie had thought about jumping in front of a train as she was on her way to our session. The message was clear and urgent. I said to the beautiful woman in front of me that I could see she was full of emotion, her mum was with her, and she had told me about the suicidal thoughts that she had almost acted on. Lizzie broke down. At the end of the session, she said her mum had saved her life and she was meant to come to me on that day. I never saw her again, but I have every hope and belief that she asked for support and has continued her precious life with her mum as her guardian angel.

With any challenging boundaries or issues that feel too hard to address on your own, or with the spiritual support I share, then I encourage, maybe urge you, to contact one of the amazing organisations out there who are ready to help, or seek professional help. I have included a few of them in the back of the book. You won't look back.

It's never too late

You are not too old, stuck in your ways, tired or any of the other reasons you may think of to explain why you wish you could set boundaries, but you can't. Neither are those around you too old, stuck in their ways or tired to take on board your boundaries either. **It is never too late to make changes in your life.**

THE ENERGY OF BROWN

Crystal: Tiger's eye is a brown and gold beauty, a foundation stone emanating grounding and strength. Keep it close to you day and night to give you the confidence and energy to build your boundaries. It is a stone of permission and encourages you to implement change. I put mine in my bra or in my pocket, so I can close my hand around it whenever I need to.

Colour: Find a brown stone or pebble to represent tiger's eye, or a piece of wood to add to your altar (more on altars and how to curate them on page 122). Breathe deeply, and as you do, visualise stepping into the cleansing colour. Look for the colour as you go about your daily life.

Affirmation:

I have put my boundaries in place.

Journal Prompt: What are my personal boundaries? How will I set them? How will I protect them?

Step 4

FINDING YOUR POTENTIAL

The pressure to earn money against the backdrop of a cost-of-living crisis is ever present. So too is the search for a fulfilling career doing something we love. Sometimes the two do not converge and we must make a decision to prioritise a regular salary over following our heart and soul's true desires. Or we take a leap of faith and change professional direction in the hope that our bold, brave move will be rewarded. Then there are the additional pressures, like juggling work and childcare, navigating a difficult office culture or dealing with redundancy – a multitude of pitfalls can distract us or change the course of our intentional path.

I never had a plan. When I talk about the journey my career has taken, I find it both hard to believe and yet completely unsurprising. I have often found myself in the right place at the right time, earning me the nickname of 'Jammy' amongst my friends, and I put this down to a blessed combination of luck and positioning, along with a little help from my spirit guides.

While my dyslexia threatened to hold me back, my strong entrepreneurial approach powered me through the highs and lows of my early working life. I have never been an employee; I have always been my own boss. From co-owning and running a bar in Tenerife in my early twenties, selling my handmade candles on a Camden market stall and giving psychic readings, to establishing a concession in Selfridges department store, founding a spiritual wellness brand and teaching people globally how to bring insight into their lives, I have done it all on my own terms. Each point on my career path has led me to the next thing, whether I have been aware of it or not, so I guess you could call it a success story, but we all know it's not as simple as that.

Our professional lives are a big part of our identity, and as much as we may try not to define ourselves by our jobs, it's often the first piece of information we give. 'So, what do you do?' we ask each other, hoping to get the measure of someone by their answer of 'accountant', 'nurse', 'retail assistant' or even 'psychic'. Although it is not foolproof, it is a quick way to find out more about them and ascertain whether someone may be clever, creative or practical, and (let's be honest) how much money they may earn.

One of the main reasons people come for a psychic reading is to find out whether they are on the right career path. They want to know what their meaningful purpose is in life and how to set the right goals and intentions to achieve this, using a variety of skills, including those we have already discussed, like confidence, intuition, manifestation and boundaries. In these sessions we call upon abundance and fulfilment through our wishes and dreams.

We also have to get real, allowing our practical head to rule as well as our intuition. Decisions around work matter, particularly those that have a financial impact – becoming freelance or running our own business – and need a heavy dose of logic as well as luck and manifestation. Without a strong and sensible foundation, a new venture is likely to struggle, because having a great idea is not always enough. And yet, when we make those big decisions and step into the unknown with our hearts and eyes open, we must not be afraid to fail.

So, how can a spiritual focus benefit us in our working life?

Step by tiny step

Do you love your job, but struggle with certain aspects of it, like the hours, your shouty boss or a difficult workmate? Or have you found yourself trudging into work wishing you could do something completely different, go back into education or realise a long-held dream? Sometimes it is hard to pinpoint what it is you are unhappy with, and it may be an aspect of your work rather than the job itself, or it could be that you are ready for a big career change. This is the point to connect with your gut instinct and ask it some searching questions to get to the root of your unease. Try the Pros and Cons exercise on page 45 or the Pendulum on page 71. We cannot make changes unless we have clarity, so we need to find out what is holding us back or making us unhappy.

Answering this question and discovering that we may be hankering after a complete change is both exciting and scary. Once we have acknowledged what it is we want to explore, then we need to construct a way of developing this other side of ourselves while continuing to work in what is currently making us money. It's a careful approach, but it allows us not to make any decisions that we may later regret.

Although my psychic ability has been with me for as long as I can remember, and I had been reading tarot for many years, I did not jump straight into earning money from my vocation. As desperate as I was to get started, I didn't assume I knew everything. Instead, I took a course in tarot reading, before establishing a development circle where I was overseen by an experienced teacher while I taught other people the power of the cards, crystals and auras. During this time, I realised how much I loved helping people tap into their intuition and how much it benefited them, and me, in the process.

I love what I do, and I can't imagine doing anything else, but there are times when I need to get back to basics, go to spiritualist church, make evening meditations my priority and remind myself of the roots of my practice. No matter how busy or successful we may become, it's important to keep learning, challenging ourselves, questioning our motivation and remembering where it all started. Factoring in a reset every now and then keeps us fresh, focused and better at what we do.

One of my clients, Teresa, was a high-powered city professional, who worked more hours than there were in a day. While she liked her job, she felt trapped on the financial hamster wheel of earning enough to pay the bills. Her dream was to retrain as a psychotherapist, but this would take several years, and she could not afford to stop working. Although she was convinced this new career was her destiny, she was shrewd enough to question what would happen if it didn't work out. What if she gave everything up and then it turned out she didn't enjoy it after all?

Teresa took small but steady steps towards her goal, starting with volunteering with the Samaritans and being accepted onto a weekend psychotherapy course, while she continued with her day job. After a couple of years, she had a qualification which allowed her to practise as a hypnotherapist, so, with a handful of clients already, she resigned from her old career. She didn't just talk about what she wished for; she made it happen. It wasn't easy, and there were times when she felt overwhelmed and torn between her existing career and the one that she was working hard to make a reality, but until she was sure she had made the right decision and was able to begin earning money, she couldn't risk making any big moves. Teresa is now a qualified psychotherapist with zero regrets.

You do not need to be stuck in anything. Keep your faith in what you want from your future, put your intention out to the universe for a different life and then to move towards your goal. Ignore those people who say you are not good enough or capable, quieten the voices that can only reiterate the negatives and let your optimism and self-belief carry you carefully and astutely forward. Start by setting an aim and giving yourself a deadline to achieve it by. Once you have reached this point, you have taken the first step to realising your dream, so set another goal. Just like climbing a steep hill, I don't look up to see how far I still have to go; I just look ahead at the path immediately in front of me. One foot in front of the other and one step at a time.

Recognising your potential

When I was in my early twenties, I knew before I received the phone call from my brother that there was bad news coming. I felt the energy and spirits flood back through the channel I had effectively blocked a decade earlier due to illness and it was a definitive sign that something was happening. I was away working in Tenerife, and I had a vision of my mum before I was told she had died. In the two days it took me to get back to the UK, grief floored me, and yet the spirit guides I had pushed away in anger during my teenage years of illness were resolutely by my side. My belief returned when I lost my mum, and I know that was not a coincidence.

I didn't want to leave my dad, so, after a brief return to Tenerife, I came back to the UK permanently. At home and unemployed, I thought hard about what I wanted to do and my potential to achieve it, and I triggered several things in quick succession. I set up a stall on Camden Market selling clothes, and I signed up for a foundation in the spiritualist church and a weekly tarot-reading course. I started buying crystals, tarot packs and making candles to sell. Through this, I began supplying a wholesaler, which encouraged me to open a little shop in Waltham Abbey. It was here that I did my first paid reading and the course of my life changed forever.

Up until this point I had only ever done readings for family and friends, but my tarot teacher said I was ready and encouraged me to take it a step further. I put a sign up in the window of the shop, offering paid readings in the back room. My first client was a guy who came in off the street, with no idea that I was just starting. I think I was charging £25, and after the reading he gave me a £50 note and told me to keep the change. I couldn't believe it! He was bowled over by his reading, telling me I was born to do it. 'This is you,' he said, like a guardian angel who had just wandered in. He didn't know me or the journey I had taken to find the thing that gave me most happiness, but he saw my potential and validated my decision. It was the confirmation I needed from the spirit world to show me that I was on the right path.

Some of us know from very young what career we want to follow, and some take a while or a roundabout route to get there. Whether we can spot the potential in ourselves or are looking for external affirmation, we need to be alert to the way markers that show us where to go.

It's okay to be ambitious

Ambition and competitiveness are often viewed as negative traits, but with the right intentions their energy is exactly what we need to push us forward. Whether you are keen to progress within an existing career or want to change direction, being ambitious will help you get there. This is not about being ruthless and you are not doing it at any cost; this is about understanding the competition you face and being ready for it. **Ambition gives us the drive and motivation to get to where we want to be, furnishing us with a sense of momentum and purpose.**

My competitiveness is only directed at myself. I use it as a measure of how well I am doing and as a way to propel me forward. As I mentioned on page 24, I plan quarterly goals which keep me focused, I plot how much I can achieve and how far I have come and set myself little challenges and manifestations. There is always a bigger plan, and when I accomplish it, I am ready to move on to the next goal.

Teamwork makes the dream work

I am always happier being part of a team. When I founded Psychic Sisters in 2006, I employed a group of women spiritualists, some of whom have been with me from the beginning. We have created a close-knit sisterhood, sharing the disappointments and celebrating the successes, and I couldn't do what I do without them. Unless you are a lone wolf, being part of a work community is an important aspect of our professional lives and we benefit from regular interaction with a group, which can be an inspiring and energising process.

Find those colleagues whose energy you connect with and create a reciprocal relationship of support and trust. **We all need a few cheerleaders, both within work and outside it.** After my appearance on BBC's *Dragons' Den*, which I will tell you more about in a bit, orders for our wellbeing products increased significantly, and it was all hands on deck to meet the response. As well as my team, some of my mates pitched in to help. A support network doesn't have to be huge; it just has to be a few people with the right intentions. The same cavalry arrived when my boyfriend, Lee, had a freak accident and broke both heels in his feet, just before Christmas, our busiest time of year. Overnight, the dominos fell and, in the morning, pals rallied around to help me pick them back up. It is at times like these that you know who your friends are, and I will never forget their generosity and selflessness.

The real relationship challenges come when we work alongside people we may not like or respect, and they could feel the same about us. There are often one or several bullies in the workplace that will push us to our limits. This is a big trigger for me and feels like being back in the playground at school. It can be hard to stand up to people in a work environment, but I have found various tricks to protect myself, which I have included on the next page.

> **SPIRITUAL TOOL: BLOCKING NEGATIVITY**
>
> I have several tools in my spiritual kit bag which I pull out when I am faced with a bully or find myself in a toxic work environment.
>
> - Kill them with kindness. This really does work. It can defuse temperamental situations and disarm difficult people but, most importantly, it protects us from being sucked into their dark vortex. It is a handy deflection, although it takes some effort, and you may feel uncomfortable or disingenuous.
>
> - The best gemstone for this situation is black obsidian, which protects us from negative energy. Put it on your desk or keep it about your person.
>
> - Create your own invisible forcefield of protection. Sit quietly, take a deep breath and begin to visualise a screen building around you and rising high above your head. Imagine this shield of armour repelling unkind comments and toxic energy. Nothing harmful can touch you.

Setting boundaries

It can be easy to forget that work is a job. No matter how crucial, necessary or life-saving your role may be, in its simplest terms, it is a way of earning money to finance the way we choose to live. Yes, it is important, but it is not our family. It is not our children. It is not our self-worth. It is not the only thing we can do with our time. Yet, it can overwhelm many of these areas unless we put healthy boundaries in place to protect our core.

We have talked about the process of setting boundaries for ourselves, and this is incredibly relevant when we are working long hours in demanding jobs. **For us to function happily, we need every area of our wellbeing – emotional, mental, physical and spiritual – to be pulling together successfully** and engendering good routines which remind us when to put our personal self before our professional one. Get up fifteen minutes earlier than you usually do and use this time for something positive and constructive, whether it is connecting to nature by wandering around your garden, doing a few stretches, putting a load of laundry on or chopping vegetables for dinner later. Do not check your emails, doomscroll or use the time in a work capacity. This is about starting your day with a productive mindset. How you start your day impacts your later self, so make the time to do something that you can be grateful for at the end of the day.

At lunchtime, make sure you take a proper break. Step away from your workspace, do not eat at your desk and, if you can, go for a walk or meet a friend for lunch. An hour of distraction is a great way to blow away the cobwebs and reset you for the afternoon. Do not work late unless it is unavoidable. Your brain will stop functioning way before you realise it has and there will be very little to be gained, unless you are the sort of person who thrives later in the day. Prioritise eating a healthy dinner, watching your favourite TV show, making time for a sport or hobby, and exercising regularly. These are all basic and practical requirements which we are often guilty of abandoning because we allow work to seep into every corner of our day and feel 'too busy', 'too stressed' or 'too tired' to carve out valuable time for ourselves away from our nine to five.

Once we have set boundaries for ourselves around work, let's think about the way we interact with colleagues. Have we fallen into a pattern of behaviour that we are not comfortable with? Perhaps we take on more work than we should or feel like we are always the one to do a certain chore when others don't take their turn. Carve out some time to pinpoint these issues firmly and fairly with your colleagues and deal with it with the kindness and respect you would expect in return. Take a proactive approach in offering a solution to the problem and be prepared to listen to any issues or ideas for positive change that they would like to raise.

A friend of mine is the only one to empty the recycling bin in the office, and it annoys him, but he doesn't say anything. He reasons that it is more than likely he does something that annoys others and there is an unspoken acceptance and compromise amongst his team. Maybe he should bring this up, but he would prefer to keep the equilibrium, believing it is easier for him to spend a few minutes emptying a bin than getting caught in a long conversation about who doesn't do what. Setting boundaries forces us to disturb the status quo and direct conversations can feel harder to have at work, but it is worth voicing your issues to avoid creeping resentment and to protect your own sense of harmony.

> **SPIRITUAL TOOL: EMOTIONAL BODY SCAN**
>
> I do this most mornings. When I wake up I lay in bed for five minutes, breathing deeply and checking in with my physical and emotional being. This is not a meditation. It is about feeling the vibrations and actively checking in with myself. Do I sense anything good or bad happening? Is my gut trying to tell me something about the day ahead? What will I be facing and is there anything I need to prepare for? I consult my mind's eye and scan through my senses. Sometimes there will be a niggle that I can't quite get to the bottom of, so I use this time to peel back the layers of emotion involved to get to the core of the issue.

Working from home

Covid changed our ways of working and forced many of us to work from home and communicate via screens rather than face to face for the first time. Lots of businesses have continued to operate in this way, and while there are positives to working remotely, the negatives can be hugely damaging for those of us who are more motivated in a busy environment, work better surrounded by colleagues or find that being at home can blur the boundaries of the beginning and end of the working day. For many, the perfect balance is to split their time between home and the office. If you do not have this option and work remotely all the time, then take it upon yourself to suggest a monthly meet-up with colleagues to help everyone feel less isolated.

There is also the issue of how working from home is perceived by those you live with and any family and friends who are close by. Sometimes the distractions are infuriating, and you can run the gauntlet of 'I have forgotten my PE kit – can you bring it to school?' or 'As you are home, would you mind giving me a hand with…' or 'I was just passing so I thought you could pop the kettle on…' Set a boundary by explaining that unless it is an emergency, you will not check your phone or answer the door until your lunch break. Just make sure you stand by this declaration and don't be tempted to respond outside of the times you set.

Creating a physical boundary is also important. If you can, set your workspace in an area that you can walk away from at the end of the day, or pack it up so you are not tempted to sit back down and continue working. Don't ever be tempted to work from the sofa or your bed unless you have no choice – these are private spaces for relaxation. Check out your local library as a potentially free and inspiring place to work for a few hours, or consider co-working with a friend in a local café every so often.

> **SPIRITUAL TOOL: SACRED WORKSPACE**
>
> Create a sacred space on your desk and surround yourself with a few choice items like a lovely family photo, scented candle, water glass, plant or flowers and a few crystals. Personalising your work area can make a big difference to how you focus on the tasks ahead, whether you are at home or in a shared office. It sets your intentions for a productive day and wards off unwanted bad energy in a bigger environment.

Taking a risk

I had the Waltham Abbey shop for a couple of years until my dad died. After the emotional upheaval of losing him, I needed a break from retail and was ready for an adventure. My boyfriend, Lee, wanted to do his PADI diving training, so we decided to go to Australia because it was cheaper to do it there and we felt like we needed to put some distance between us and home. I can work anywhere, so we decided to go for three months. When we arrived in Cairns, I went to the local spiritualist centre in case they needed any temporary readers, and one of the friendly staff said, 'Can you start now?!' Someone had just called, desperate for a reading, and there was nobody available. I had a job!

The team at the centre were fantastic and invited me to join them on an Australian psychic expo tour for a few months. This was a great opportunity, except we were due to fly home. Lee had to go back to the UK, but he said I should go for it. I made a quick decision and took the gamble to stay in Australia. It turned out to be the right choice. The team were lovely, really looked out for me and I was fortunate enough to be asked to go on radio and TV to talk about my work. Taking the risk paid off. I grew a lot both personally and professionally, pushed myself outside of my comfort zone and was even able to hire a car and drive to some incredible places that I otherwise wouldn't have experienced, like Mount Isa, right in the middle of the Outback. When I came back home several months later, my perspective on my job had changed and I was ready to take my career to the next stage.

Over the years, I have often been in the right place at the right time. This is partly due to luck, but I think it is also about where my spirit guide, Star, positions me in life and what I am open to. I am not fearless, but I do push myself and take risks, accepting that sometimes things may go wrong. We all need a little bravery to push us out of our comfort zone and recognise opportunities as they arise. **Sometimes, saying 'yes' is the key to unlocking the next door.**

Let fate play a part

When I came back from Australia, I could feel the energies shifting purposefully around me, but I was not sure what the result would be. I was renting rooms for readings and many of my old clients returned along with a big influx of new people. I had a magazine column, I was on TV in *The Psychic Show*, and I was doing guest appearances on mainstream programmes like *This Morning*. My career was going well and I loved spreading the spiritual word. I wasn't actively thinking about expansion or world domination, but every so often I would daydream out loud to Lee, and I mentioned the idea of getting a concession in Selfridges. He thought it would be a big mistake because it would mean I was tied down to a retail space again, and because both of us loved travelling, we wanted to retain the freedom to be able to do more of it.

I popped into Selfridges at Christmas and bought a gift pack of Aveda goodies. When I got home, I realised one of the items – peppermint foot gel, which I really wanted to try – was missing, so I had to go back. I was meeting a friend for lunch and suggested going to the store so I could kill two birds with one stone. It was as mundane a decision as that. We were in the café in Selfridges and were tucked in a corner so I could give her a discreet reading, when I was aware that someone was staring at me from a distance. A smartly dressed gentleman was standing in the café next to a woman he kept turning to, before looking back at me. As a joke, I said to my friend that that was the man I needed to talk to about getting a concession in the store. She laughed, but I could feel a weird connection.

The man in the suit came over and asked what I was doing, and I explained I was giving a reading. We had the funniest conversation, with lots of banter, and I could feel the shared energy between us before he introduced himself. It turned out he was the managing director of Selfridges, Paul Kelly, and, unbeknownst to me, he walked the floor every Tuesday for an hour or so. Fate had positioned me once again. He turned to the woman he was with and said, 'I want her in my store!' That was how it happened. In that moment, everything came together, and within a couple of meetings and several months, I had secured a concession in Selfridges.

Lee advised me against doing it. I could see his point, but if Selfridges was taking a risk with me, the least I could do was give it my best shot. I had some stock left over from the Waltham Abbey shop, I bought a mobile phone and a few IKEA bookcases, spending less than £300 in total. The friend I was with in the café that fortuitous day had become my new business partner, and we were ready to start our exciting venture. The day before we were due to move into the store, I became ill and my arms and legs were spasming, so I was rushed to hospital in an ambulance. The doctors thought I might have a brain tumour and I was booked in for a scan the following morning – when I should have been arriving at Selfridges. Instead, my business partner was there and having issues getting in because nobody had been told we were turning up that day. She rang me and said she couldn't do it. I thought she meant she couldn't access the store, but no, she said she didn't want to be part of the business and she was leaving before we had even got started. I was stuck in a hospital bed unable to do anything and waiting for what could have been life-changing news. Luckily, it turned out to be a trapped nerve in my spine and I was sent home the next day.

I went straight to Selfridges to finish setting up the space on my own.

Lee was my rock. As much as he had advised me against taking on this challenge, the moment he knew I was serious, he wholeheartedly supported me. He was the one that came up with the name 'Psychic Sisters', which perfectly summed up the small group of spiritual women I had gathered together to work with me. We screened off private spaces to give readings, set up a few shelves of wellbeing products to sell, and we hit the ground running. There was no marketing team, brand advisers or PR people, just Lee and I working on gut instinct and with a careful eye on the finances.

If you have a deep passion, an undeniable talent or a burning ambition for something you believe in, then go for it. No matter how tough things get, this is what will sustain you in the dark, anxious hours in the middle of the night. You need to truly believe in what you do, grasp it with both hands and keep going. That's what I did. I built something from nothing and if it all breaks down, I know I can do it again. Fate played a part along with a vision, hard graft and unflinching commitment. We have been in Selfridges for almost twenty years, and the company have been phenomenal. They have supported us throughout and regularly show how much they value us as part of their store family. It's one of the best career decisions I have made and I always say I will be there until the day I die.

Know your weaknesses

Understanding where your weaknesses are in your professional life is not a negative. It requires transparency and acceptance to pinpoint what you may need to change, adapt or work harder on. As someone with dyslexia, I can have fifty different things pinging around in my brain during one thought process. I find it hard to fully focus on something, without it being crowded by lots of other ideas, so I am always finding ways to calm my scatty mind. Having my own business is both good and bad for my dyslexic capabilities, but I can't imagine doing anything else. One of the important tricks I use is to treat myself as an employee of my own business, visualising stepping out of my body and sitting opposite myself to appraise my performance. I need to come under as much scrutiny as other areas of my company. This really works and gives me the clarity I need, playing a trick with my brain, which sends it into professional mode and gets good results. Try it. Imagine splitting yourself in two, the professional and the personal, and allow the first voice to take charge, being as unbiased as possible. Raise the points a boss would make and then allow your second voice to respond to this, trying to be as objective as possible. Make notes on behalf of both voices to see what changes may need to be made.

I regularly check in with myself. A while ago, finding myself spiralling towards burnout, I knew I had to take drastic action. One of the things I did was step back from giving readings every day, as the workload and pressure I was under was immense. I cast a critical eye over the situation and decided to swap one of my tarot-reading days with being in the warehouse and working on my products. This is the part of my job that I love, and I realised I wasn't doing enough of it. It gave me an opportunity to breathe and be creative, which in turn fuelled my passion and commitment for my client days. Now I have a better balance in every area of my work.

Stepping out of your comfort zone

I had watched *Dragons' Den* for years and always wanted to do it. Lee said I didn't need to, the business was going really well, but the idea bubbled away in the back of my mind. I mentioned it to a friend and, in the process of discussing it, I set the intention by saying it out loud, before going home, googling the programme and finding an application form online. A few weeks later I had a call from one of the producers while I was out shopping in M&S. He asked me lots of questions, we had a good chat and he said he would be back in touch in the next few months. He rang back within a couple of hours to say I had made it through to the second stage!

I had to submit a video of myself chatting about my business and then we went through the due diligence and legalities, before they confirmed I was on the programme. I was so thrilled, but also nervous that my dyslexia would trip me up, and so I asked Grace, an actress friend, if she would come onto the show with me. We got the call on the Thursday and by the following Tuesday we were in Manchester, ready to film. I did my moon magic spell before I left, manifesting four Dragons but focusing on two.

I wasn't nervous walking into the room and facing the Dragons; I was just so happy to finally be there. I had citrine for better intuition and green aventurine crystals to relax me tucked into my bra; I was ready for this. Grace and I started our pitch, and it flowed so well until the microphones inexplicably cut out, so we had to stop and start again. Sara Davies, one of the Dragons, made eye contact with me and was smiling encouragingly, and I thought, *I really like you.* By the end of the pitch, amazingly I had offers from four Dragons, but I had the strongest connection with Sara, so I knew the decision I was going to make.

SPIRITUAL TOOL: MOON MAGIC SPELL

First, you need a full moon! This is the best time to set your intentions. Choose your crystal. Before I went on *Dragons' Den*, I did this exercise using citrine for intuition and abundance and green aventurine to keep me calm and boost my confidence. On a piece of paper, write down your intention. I wrote: 'I have two investors, four offers.' You can choose to write more than one, maybe a list of four or eight manifestations you want to focus on between full moons. I didn't want to muddle anything before the TV programme, so I kept my spell focused. If you can, go outside and look up to the moon, or sit inside by a window. Hold the gemstones in your hand and say in your head or out loud, 'I call upon the power of the moon to set my intention to my spell.' Say this mantra eight times before wrapping the paper around the crystals, take a deep breath and say, 'So mote it be' (an ancient phrase meaning 'so may it be'). Hold it for a few minutes, breathe in your heart's desire and exhale it to the full moon. Visualise yourself doing your intention. I imagined myself walking into the Den and the Dragons making an offer, watching it play out in my mind's eye. With the intention, I either keep it wrapped around the crystals and in a drawer until next full moon, or I unwrap it and burn the paper. I did this for my *Dragons' Den* intention and put the crystals back in my bowl of many gemstones.

Having a mentor and being one

One of the most appealing aspects of taking part in *Dragons' Den* was the possibility of working closely with one of the Dragons. Having a mentor or guide, no matter how successful we may be in our career, creates a safe, protective, honest and inspiring relationship to thrive from. As a business owner, a mentor makes me feel less alone and gives me direction and a sounding board, but you don't need to run your own company to qualify for one. There are mentors and coaches for all areas of life and those who specialise in careers – if you work for a large corporation, you may already have access to them – or you can create your own support system. I am part of a network of women in business who gather regularly to discuss issues, share connections and hold each other up in difficult times. It's a powerful and inspirational circle, another vital sisterhood in my life along with my Psychic Sisters team.

I am also a mentor for big businesses and work closely with several global brands behind the scenes, advising on scheduling, employee recruitment and other practical aspects. Taking a spiritual approach to decision-making is vital and has a significant impact on the success of the company. I was working with an international client who was in the process of buying a large hotel. They sent me the details and, while it needed complete refurbishment, it looked good on paper. My intuition immediately pulled up an issue with the foundations of the building, and I told my client this was a major problem and to think twice before proceeding. They thought I was mistaken after an early investigation had not shown any problems, but after spending a significant sum on foundation tests they discovered a severe and costly issue which would have cost them millions to put right. They pulled out of the deal.

As well as companies, I work with individuals on their professional decisions. An actor client of mine had been offered a film role and was about to accept it. During a reading for him, I knew it was going to be a flop and would affect his career, so I shared this. He didn't want to know, citing the amount of money he would make and the need to keep working. He took the job. From the day he arrived on set, everything went wrong and the film didn't make cinematic release. It took him a long time to recover from the disappointment.

Finding someone who can give us a professional pep talk now and again, and being able to reciprocate this to others, is one of the ways we can build a happier, more productive outlook in our working life.

Coping with burnout

I see this amongst some of my clients who relentlessly push themselves professionally, working harder and longer hours, until something snaps. I think it is a place we have all been in or hover near at various points in our lives. Suddenly, small everyday things become big mountains to climb, and we are continually overwhelmed by life. **As much as our natural drive and determination will expect us to keep going, we must stop.** The biggest problem is admitting to ourselves and those around us that we need to rest. At this point, teetering on the edge of illness, we have no option but to put ourselves first and listen to our intuitive voice telling us what we need, so allow it the space and quiet to speak. This has happened for a reason, and we need to take heed. It's a big wake-up call, whether your burnout is telling you that you love what you do but need to reevaluate how you do it, or it is indicating that you are not where you really want to be. In the next step we look at all the positive moves you can make to re-energise your mind, body and soul.

Asking for abundance

I regularly use affirmations, manifestations and moon magic spells around career developments and decision-making and then, at the end of each month, I send a simple message to the universe. I thank it for the brilliant things that have come my way over previous weeks, I acknowledge the lessons I need to learn, and I ask for abundance. This is not a specific request, just recognition that in everything I do, I hope to reap the rewards tenfold, whether this is in my professional life, emotional journey, physical health or spiritual enlightenment. It is both a good place to end the month and a springboard to bounce off into the new one.

THE ENERGY OF TRANSLUCENCE

Crystal: Clear quartz is one of the gemstones that gives greater clarity to our thought process. It opens the mind's eye and carries an inner vibration which promotes awareness and transparency in every part of our emotional, physical and spiritual being. It focuses on our potential and encourages freedom. I think of it as the 'Go Get' crystal or the 'I Can' stone.

Clear quartz is associated with the crown chakra, which links it to mindfulness and higher levels of consciousness. For a five-minute meditation, sit quietly, place the crystal on your head or hold it in your hand and allow your mind to empty. As thoughts ping back in, push them away again and focus solely on the clear quartz. Alternatively, place it on your bedside table or under your pillow before you go to sleep.

Colour: Instead of a crystal, you could use a piece of sea glass or visualise something that makes you feel clearer and calmer. It doesn't have to be a colour; it can be a thing of clarity that can support us.

Affirmation:

I am reaching my potential.

Journal Prompt: Where would I like my potential to take me? How can I help this process?

ENLIGHTENMENT

Step 5

YOUR INNER GODDESS

Now we journey into the second half of the book and look more closely at the intentional stages of healing, cleansing and nourishment. There is no better place to start than with awakening our inner goddess.

When we think of a goddess, we may imagine the exalted, sacred beings who flit through the mythical stories of ancient civilisations or appear as pagan deities, encapsulating universal characteristics like creation, healing, peace, love and fertility, which tempers the gods who focus on war, weather and fate. In the present day, we use the word to describe a female celebrity who appears untouchable or refer to a wonderful friend as a 'goddess', but what about the feminine deity we hold inside us?

A nurturing and liberating presence, **the inner goddess represents our divine femininity and hidden self** and empowers us to reach out beyond what we think is possible to harness our potential. By galvanising our external masculine strength and igniting our internal feminine power, we call upon her to bring balance and fulfilment in our life. She is waiting for you.

My interpretation and beliefs focus primarily on my inner goddess, but I also rely on the deep connections I have to spiritual goddesses through my tarot cards, and I utilise their collective energy. This is a different relationship from the one I have with my spirit guides. My guides speak to me from the spirit world, they represent an external communication that arrives through an open channel, whereas my inner goddess is internal, held in the core of my being, and I access her power on a different wavelength. I work with one or the other depending on what I am facing, but I need my inner goddess every day. Breathing her energy in and exhaling her purity, I rely on the combination of strident masculine vibrations and spiritual feminine verve, and I call upon her whenever I need a little extra help.

Connecting with our goddess means finding our true self, the child we were, the innocence we carried, the kindness we showed to ourselves. The goddess banishes negative thoughts and self-criticism, gives us permission to counteract and dispel the difficult parts of who we are and softens our hard edges. She leads us to empathy and tranquillity and connects us to the universe. Like a light switch you can turn on when you need to, she radiates confidence, control and peace. She is you and she is not you, she is an enlightened being channelling her divine power and cyclical energy to inspire intuition and freedom.

As I was writing this chapter, I realised how disconnected I had become from my inner goddess and that my spirit guides have been at the fore instead. I had been too busy and too distracted and allowed myself to lose sight of her. As I worked, I sensed her nudging me through the words and exercises I was noting down, directing me towards those to include and reminding me I needed to reconnect with her before I told others what to do. I started each day with an exercise to reawaken my bond with my inner goddess, which she wants me to pass on to you.

SPIRITUAL TOOL:
ACTIVATE YOUR INNER GODDESS

Stand barefoot on the grass, feet hip-width apart, rooted to the ground. Spread your toes, balance your weight evenly and feel the cool earth under your feet. Drop your shoulders, relax your body, close your eyes and focus on the point of connection where your body and the earth meet. Now take a deep breath in and, as you do, imagine drawing Mother Earth's vibrations from the ground, upward through the soles of your feet. Let them travel to your knees, through your thighs and up to your root chakra at the base of your spine. Feel the energy and light moving through the cells of your body as it cleanses and clears your pathways. Send it to each of your other chakras; sacral below your navel, solar plexus in your stomach, heart, throat, third eye in the middle of your forehead and crown at the top of the head. Now release

> your breath slowly and push the energy back down to the earth. Our inner goddess has a close relationship with Mother Earth, so this is a good meditation to use to open those channels and strengthen your bond with your divine feminine powers.

Acceptance of who we are

One of the central roles of our inner goddess is to remind us how fabulous we are. She transcends negativity and self-hatred and shows us there is a different way to be. Rather than focusing on our physical and emotional imperfections, she encourages us to celebrate the positives, the parts of us we are proud of. You may not like the shape of your nose, but look at your fantastic legs! Okay, so you hate the way you cry easily, but how wonderful to be in touch with your emotions! Thinking we are not good enough becomes a self-fulfilling prophecy and creates a spiral of behaviour that damages our confidence and capabilities. It supresses our inner goddess, robbing her of her voice and energy at the point we need her most. **Would we talk to others the way we often speak to ourselves?** No. Think of this when your internal voice reprimands you and replace 'I can't' with 'I can'. Every time you begin a negative thought or voice a pessimistic attitude, visualise your goddess rising up and breathing positivity into your heart and soul to re-energise your spirit.

Acceptance of who we are can feel like an impossible goal, and there are times when it is easier to attain than others. It doesn't mean that we stop looking after ourselves and stay on the sofa eating chocolate digestives every night; it is about understanding who we really are. Here's a truthful insight into my approach to it, and it may surprise you. While I wholeheartedly accept who I am, I am open about the plastic surgery I have had. I don't do it because of pressure from society or fear of getting older; I do it for myself. This is part of my quest to take care of myself, and while it is a small part, I think it is significant, and that's important to share with you. It is right for me, and it makes me happy. That said, I have no qualms turning up to a business meeting in leggings, trainers and unwashed hair scraped back in a ponytail. I do not want to be disrespectful to the people I am meeting, but I don't force myself to make a big effort with my appearance if I don't feel like it. I take confidence from my inner goddess and think what matters most is who I am as a person, not what I look like.

SPIRITUAL TOOL: ENERGY CLEARING

This is a practice which could sit anywhere in this book, but I like the fact that my inner goddess has indicated for me to put it here. If ever in doubt, a little energy clearing with a sage stick can make all the difference.

You can buy one or make your own sage stick by

> growing sage and cutting a bunch of leaves. You may want to add other herbs like lavender or rosemary, but I like the purity of sage on its own. Tie the bunch together by winding string from the bottom to the top of the bundle and back again, securing with a knot. Now hang the stick somewhere like a warm airing cupboard or in the sun, to dry out, which should take a week or so. When you are ready, light the tip of the stick and let it burn for a moment before blowing it out and moving the smoke around. As you do so, repeat the affirmation, 'My space is cleansed, protected, and free of negative energy.'
>
> **NB**: If you can't burn sage sticks because of smoke alarms, try sage oil instead, putting a few drops onto an oil burner.

Daydreams and doodles

While at night our dreams bubble up from our subconscious, full of snippets from our memory banks and data our brain is still filing away, our daydreams come from our conscious desires. Dreaming in the day is a lost art now we have mobile phones we can scroll through when we are on the bus, waiting in a queue or sitting in the doctor's reception, so we must actively make time for it. This is one of the channels our inner goddess will use to reach us. Take ten minutes out, sit somewhere you won't be disturbed, preferably near a window with a view, which can help you drift into a daydream. **Play around with your thoughts, think about your deepest desires and visualise new ideas and directions to take.** Don't think about solutions to problems, a list of admin you need to get through or what to buy in the supermarket later – this is time for your mind to run free through meadows of possibility.

You may want to pick up a pen and paper to doodle as you daydream, writing words that come into your head or letting your hand freestyle sketches and shapes. Ask your inner goddess to communicate with you through your mind's eye. Perhaps she will give you an affirmation for the day, so let your subconscious flow. Sit back and look at what you have put down on paper – it could be illuminating.

SPIRITUAL TOOL: DIAGNOSING DOODLES

I doodle all the time. If I am in a meeting or on a phone call with someone, I will do it subconsciously and then I look at the results to find out what my goddess or spirit guides may be telling me. I have learned to recognise what certain symbols mean to me, so here are my top eight doodles and their interpretations.

Pentagrams: This is the symbol I use to instil calm. It also signifies creative vision and perfection. I see this and I know I am on the right track.

Pentagrams with circles: As above, but also includes protection.

Stars: Everything is aligned.

Circles: A symbol of frustration to me!

Squares: A series of squares or boxes will indicate my need for organisation and structure or represent building a wall of protection.

Flowers: Indicates multiple things I need to do and calls for organisation.

Triangles: Peaks of balance, unity and inner confidence. A symbol of friendship and celebration.

Infinity: This symbol is ever moving, depicting the spiritual flow.

Cleansing our inner goddess

Our inner goddess is closely aligned with Mother Earth and both divine energies converge through the seasons, the moon cycle and nature's vibrations to give us strength, balance and healing. I particularly love the intense magic of the moon, as a pure channel from the spirit which has helped me through emotional and physical challenges and times of change, and I talk about this in more detail in the next chapter. For my inner goddess, I use the full moon to cleanse and revitalise her energy, turning her towards the moon's mesmeric nocturnal light. There are myriad ways to practise moon bathing.

- Stand outside, in the light of the full moon, look up and repeat your affirmation: 'I absorb the energy of the moon and bring positive power into my life.'
- If you are near the sea, get into the water under a full moon. Feel the tidal vibrations wash over you and send your intentions out across the ocean with the moon as your witness.
- If you can't go outside, pay homage to the moon goddesses by lighting three candles to represent the pagan deities and invite them to connect to your inner goddess.
- Leave an amethyst crystal on the windowsill to cleanse and recharge in the light of the full moon.

Strike a (yoga) pose

Yoga is an ancient practice combining physical and spiritual disciplines focusing on meditation, breathwork and movement. It can improve our balance, flexibility and strength, as well as promote relaxation, clarity and calm. The self-awareness it brings makes this an unbeatable exercise for connecting with our inner goddess. There is even a position called Goddess Pose.

The beginner-level Goddess Pose is a squat, which echoes the position of the Goddess Kali, who was known for summoning fierce feminine energy. It is also part of the moon salutation, which resonates with me. Targeting the hips and pelvis, the pose helps with menstruation, labour and hormonal issues, and the positioning of the arms releases emotional and physical tightness held in the hips, pelvis and lower back. This position exudes positivity and fights negative energy.

Whether you are a yoga devotee or a curious newcomer, introduce the Goddess Pose into your routine or start the day with a few repetitions of it. Take your feet out wide and sit down into a deep but comfortable squat, knees apart, feet planted firmly into the ground. Shoulders down, raise your arms by your side and bend your elbows, palms facing forwards. Hold the position for several deep breaths. While this is a straightforward pose, it is important not to attempt it without the proper understanding of how to do it, so this is a description rather than an instruction.

SPIRITUAL TOOL: BUILD AN ALTAR

Build an altar for your inner goddess, preferably on your bedside table so it is the first thing you see when you wake and the last thing you look at before you sleep. Whatever you choose to include should reflect your goddess and appeal to your senses. Maybe a plant or a posy of flowers, essential oils, books, candles and your crystals. Change things around if an element doesn't inspire you or if you discover an item you want to include. I always keep an eye out for feathers, and I add them to my altar, or I give them to my friend who also loves feathers, to include in her display. If this is something you know others do, then take a gift around for their altar.

Find your tribe

When we first meet people, I believe our inner goddesses connect before we are consciously aware we will build a relationship with someone. Like a clashing of cymbals, it is the coming together of energies which can either result in a happy friendship or the certainty that we do not want to spend time with that person. We can have a physical reaction to strangers, a magnetic pull towards or a repellent push away from them, and we get better at paying attention to this as we get older and gain more life experience. I have a buzzy energy which can make me a bit of a people magnet. It often opens something in others, whether it is an emotional response or a boost in their mood, and I will angle and adapt my energy accordingly. I have also learned to expertly deflect any negativity. Surrounding ourselves with like-minded people is empowering, uplifting and an utter joy.

My inner goddess has brought people to me, particularly the amazing group of women I work with, who are an integral part of Psychic Sisters. Like Sheila, who was working on one of the make-up counters in Selfridges and would pop down to my concession when she was on her break. We would chat and, while we did, she would pick up crystals and hold them in her hand. One day I gave her a reading and said, 'Sheila, you are going to work with us, you will read for me.' She didn't believe me at first, but a few months later she joined Psychic Sisters, started reading and has never looked back. She didn't know she had the gift, but I see it in people, and it was strong in her. She had found her place. And Jackie, who came in for a reading, and when she sat down in front of me, I knew I was going to offer her a job. I told her she didn't need a reading; she was going to work with me instead. The poor woman had already paid and was not expecting her career to turn around in an instant, but that is what happened. Sixteen years later, she is still working with me and still hasn't had her reading!

Then there is Carole. We met through a Botox clinic I went to and she was working in the building. She had a terrible boss and was really unhappy, but I didn't know until I gave her a reading how stuck she was in a toxic situation. 'You are going to come and work with me,' I told her. 'I don't have a job for you, but I will find one.' Carole came to be our receptionist before becoming a reader, and she is a brilliant one. She says she has found her family. That's how our sisterhood feels, like a wonderful group of goddesses who have found each other against the odds. And there are men who join us too, like my boyfriend, Lee, who runs the warehouse, and my friend Peter, who joins our social outings, as well as other friends who we refer to as the 'outer sisterhood'.

Spending time with the people we love nourishes us and blows away the cobwebs of complacency. It is also the best fun. Carole and Jackie often come out to LA with me for work events and we have such a laugh. On one occasion, we were giving readings at an A-list movie star's house with a group of his celebrity friends. I went to the loo and the door stuck so I couldn't get out and had to try to attract Carole's attention to rescue me. Later in the day we were taking a break in the kitchen there and Carole started to do the washing up! The actor told her to stop because he had a housekeeper who would tidy. As we left, he walked us down the drive to the big electric gates, which swung open as the bus that took tours around celebrity homes in the neighbourhood drove slowly past and all the passengers jumped up to take photographs of us all.

They also joined me when we took part in a programme about Hollywood psychics and filmed a pilot for Paramount. We had a buggy to race around the studio in and one very hot day, Carole and I drove it to the waterfall in the middle of the studio lot, took our shoes off and paddled in the decorative waterfall there.

We have many happy memories, with many more to make. I am so grateful to my inner goddess for bringing these amazing people into my life and I am lucky that we work together and see each other every day. If you have a sisterhood you don't see regularly, then why not set up a WhatsApp group of support and affirmation. Share your inner goddess with someone who needs a little extra magic, healing wishes or a power boost.

Everyone else can join in on the message with their own goddess inspiration.

Mythic goddesses, assemble!

In my work with tarot, as well as doing readings, I have produced my own specially commissioned decks, inspired by leading spiritual powers like the moon, angels and crystals. I love them all, but the cards I am often drawn to are the mythic goddesses, a gathering of heavenly deities from different cultures and beliefs who I have invited to come together in one tarot pack. Their sacred femininity, coupled with the spiritual power of the cards, adds a divine dimension to the tarot practice.

I know the idea of tarot cards can make people feel uneasy or scared. Some think they are linked to Ouija boards and once the channel to the spirit world is open it is impossible to shut down, resulting in bad spirits being unleashed. This is not the case. I am not here to make you do anything you are not comfortable with, but I do want to challenge your preconceptions on this journey and encourage you to step outside your comfort zone. If you have not had a tarot reading before or played around with a set of cards, then this may be the moment. I always recommend having a tarot reading from a reputable psychic who is able to steer you through the process, connect to the spirits and translate the meaning. However, as an introduction to tarot, a gentler start can be to get your own deck of cards which you can take time to get to know. They come with a manual to refer to, but don't be too rigid around the detailed meaning of each card. Play around with them. I know this may seem like a strange idea, but you are in control and need to take your time understanding your deck before you begin reading.

I am often asked how to get started with tarot readings and I always suggest beginning with a one-card pull. Shuffle the pack, pick a card and refer to the instruction book that comes with them to get to know the card a little better. Once you feel well acquainted with the deck, you are ready to move on to the three-card spread, which is simple and effective and can give you more insight without overwhelming or confusing you. This affords a good overview of what is going on for you at that time.

Lay the three cards out and read from left to right. The first card can symbolise the Past, the next is the Present and the third is the Future. Alternatively, you could read them as Situation, Obstacle and Advice, or Mind, Body and Spirit. Once you have finished your reading, shuffle the pack and knock three times on top of the deck to clear the old energy. I will also pop a couple of crystals on top of the pack and leave for several hours. From here, you can eventually move on to six-card and then nine-card readings. (See page 206 for a more detailed explanation of tarot reading.)

I always have a tarot deck with me, whether it's in my handbag, the glovebox of my car, in meetings or at home. I instinctively reach for them when I need them, like I will do with crystals, feeling the security of just holding the pack.

INTENTIONAL LIVING

SPIRITUAL TOOL: TAROT CARDS

There will be times when you feel you cannot reach your inner goddess, or that she is fading and needs to be brought back to strength and good health. Time for the cavalry! Turn to page 230 and choose a mythical goddess from my own tarot deck for an additional injection of power and love, or pull out eight goddess-inspired cards from a pack you already have.

Rhiannon: Judgement

Meaning: Inner calling
Key words: Healing, change, focus, rebirth
Affirmation:

I am focused on the choices I make.

Lakshmi: The World

Meaning: Achievement
Key words: Prosperity, ending, movement, new beginnings
Affirmation:

I am successful in everything I do.

Magec: The Sun

Meaning: Joy
Key words: Emotional wealth, joy, confidence
Affirmation:

I am happy in myself and grounded in the world around me.

Selene: The Moon

Meaning: Illusion
Key words: Intuition, uplifting, reflective
Affirmation:

I see the light through the darkness.

Asase Yaa: The Empress

Meaning: Abundance
Key words: Motherhood, fertility, nurture, honesty
Affirmation:

I am grounded and surrounded by abundance.

Elpis: The Star

Meaning: Hope
Key words: Dreams, ambition, belief
Affirmation:

I believe in everything I do.

Juno: The Hierophant

Meaning: Spiritual wisdom
Key words: Knowledge, companionship, spirituality
Affirmation:

I am open to learning.

Tyche: The Wheel of Fortune

Meaning: Destiny
Key words: Movement, luck, transformation
Affirmation:

I am moving freely.

Ma'at: The Emperor

Meaning: Authority
Key words: Legality, balance, justice, decisions
Affirmation:

I make my own decisions and trust my intuition.

Inner goddess gathering

Whether you find something local to you, or you decide to create your own gathering, **there can be nothing more powerful than a group of like-minded people coming together in celebration and discovery.** This could be mixed-gender, designed to create a spiritual community and build a strong, supportive network, or it can be female-focused, maybe for those on a quest to find or encourage their inner goddess through the empowerment of the sisterhood. Gatherings can be anything from a chat over coffee to weekly yoga sessions or going away on a retreat. I know of many approaches, including dancing workshops, woodland sound baths, beach meditations and yoga weekends.

Water is a wonderful way to connect with others, and wild swimming has become hugely popular in recent years. There are also saunas popping up on beaches around the UK coastline which offer the fantastic experience of cleansing heat followed by a bracing dip in the sea. (I talk about cold water therapy more on page 140.)

A friend of mine tapped into her inner goddess by going to a female-only sweat lodge. Sweat lodges were traditional to the Indigenous peoples of the Americas, before their popularity spread. There are strict requirements for Elders who lead the lodge to have been through many years of rigorous training because of the possible emotional and physical dangers involved. In its basic form, a lodge is a little like the skeleton of a low yurt, which is then overlaid with many blankets to keep the heat in. A hole is dug in the middle of the lodge and the door faces a large, flaming firepit several feet away where rocks are heated and then dropped into the hole. The heat builds to create a scorching, steamy environment where the semi-naked group assemble to sweat out impurities and take part in a series of chants, mantras and confessions to enable spiritual cleansing and a deeper connection to themselves, their ancestors and the universe.

My friend was fascinated by her sweat lodge experience but did not feel she was in the most trustworthy hands, as emotions ran high and were not properly addressed, several attendees had to take on roles they were not equipped for and there was no safe space for escape or follow-up support. The last thing I want to do is put you off in your search for spiritual awakening, but this underlines how important it is to research these types of gatherings and to be sure it is a responsibly run event that you are emotionally prepared for.

THE ENERGY OF PURPLE

Crystal: Amethyst is a crystal to access the mind's eye, bring the holder in touch with the divine, bolster intuition and radiate peace. It absorbs negative energy.

Colour: Purple is connected to the crown chakra and is significant in ecclesiastical, regal and spiritual events. In the aura it denotes enlightenment.

Affirmation:

I call upon my inner goddess to protect and guide me.

Journal Prompt: Can I describe the attributes of my inner goddess? What are the best ways for me to connect with her?

Step 6

RECHARGE AND EMBRACE REST

In our fast-moving daily lives, it can be considered weak to want to take a step back, and making time for rest can feel like something we have to earn the right to do. However, we must be acutely aware of what happens if we don't prioritise recharging our emotional and physical batteries. It is easy to become overwhelmed by the demands of work, family and loved ones, financial stresses, health issues and our own expectations of ourselves. Almost without realising, we can find ourselves exhausted and drained by a fatigue that it is impossible to soothe with just a good night's sleep. Putting it bluntly, before we know it, we are heading towards the serious state of burnout, which can then lead to a full emotional, mental, physical and spiritual breakdown.

The first change we must make is to recognise when everything is becoming too much before it swallows us whole. This is a work in progress for me. I check in on myself on a weekly basis, through meditation, journalling and manifestation, but as I've already mentioned, I can still get caught out and I know exactly where my tipping point is. It is the moment I begin to fantasise about getting on a plane on my own and travelling a long, long way from home. From nowhere, I yearn for a break, not a weekend away, but a dramatic escape, and then I know I have pushed myself too far. At this point, I make some changes to my lifestyle. They do not have to be severe, but they do need to have an immediate impact.

Taking time out isn't always about taking a day off; it's about a fundamental reset in every aspect of our lives. Asking the question, 'What do you do in your spare time?' sounds dated and irrelevant, in an age where many of us have blurred boundaries around our working lives. Who has time to spare these days? Well, all of us should. And time that we are not working isn't spare – it's precious.

Stepping away from everything and finding space for ourselves has a huge impact on our physical health, lowers our blood pressure and helps us recover from illness and injury. It is also crucial for our mental health and wellbeing, helping us to tackle stress and anxiety, boost our positivity and build our strength and resilience to face challenges. Put like that, it sounds just as important to put ourselves first as it is to maintain our home life and hold down a job.

One of the quickest ways for me to recalibrate my day is to spend time, as you already know, in nature. So much of our lives involves dashing from one place to the next and staring down at our feet or a phone screen, that we miss much of what is around us. When I walk through the fields near where I live, I go and say hello to the horses and I look up at the trees, birds and cloud formations. When I am in the city, I pay attention to the details we can often miss and marvel at the incredible architecture. We are surrounded by such beauty – natural and manmade – and taking the time to pause and appreciate the world around us can help us to feel more present and remind us, in a good way, how small and insignificant we are in the world. Here are some ideas on how to seek solace and rest from the tough realities of life and always remember to stop and say hello to the horses.

Being in nature

How often do you truly immerse yourself in the natural world? If you have a garden, make the most of it. And if you don't have outside space, then sit on the front doorstep with your cuppa and watch the world go by or take a sandwich to your local park bench. There are also amazing community projects in green spaces who are often looking for volunteers and local allotments that have a waiting list you can add your name to. In the meantime, there may be a friend or elderly neighbour who needs a hand in their veg patch. Wherever we live, there is always a patch of green nearby or a place we can visit, whether we want to get involved in its upkeep or not. I am constantly amazed by the diverse foliage that pops up in the city if you know where to look; the wild garlic in woody glades, blackberries sprawled along the railway cutting, large urban parklands and ancient oaks for shade.

Many of us are just a short train or bus journey away from striding through wetlands, picnicking by riverbanks, looking for mushrooms in woodlands and hunting for sea glass on the beach. Don't plug in your earphones; enjoy your rural adventure with the diverse sounds of a wild backdrop. If you ever feel overwhelmed by life, then lying in a field watching the clouds float by or standing on the shoreline and looking out across a vast ocean shows our insignificance in a life-affirming way. **Nature is an instant salve.**

Every season brings its own joys for me. In the summer, I wish I could catch the poetic beauty of first light and the hopeful sunrise, but I am not an early riser. Instead, once I am out of bed, I have a daily routine of filling the bird feeder and then making myself a coffee. While I drink it, I watch the birds arriving for breakfast. I take every opportunity to be outside on warm, sunny days. I feel like a battery being recharged by the sun, ready to power me through the long winter ahead.

I love the winter too and I embrace the change of seasons and the shift in energy. I like proper cold and snowy climes, lazing in front of log fires, lighting candles, hot baths with essential oils, snuggling in bed and the comfort food of stews and pies. Practising a seasonal approach to the year helps me accept the speed at which time travels and reminds me that nothing is forever, good or bad. We are continually moving.

Harnessing the power of the natural world

I will often choose an object from nature to act as a talisman for specific moments in my life. It reminds me of when I was a child and in a desperate search for a four-leaf clover. I spent hours with my face pressed into the grass with no joy, so one day I picked a three-leaf clover, glued it to a piece of card and stuck an extra leaf on. I remember my dad laughing a lot at that. I still haven't found one, but I know people who have, so never give up looking! Whether it is a four-leaf clover or any other natural item which may signify something to you, these can be just as powerful as the crystals we use.

A friend went to a funeral in a beautiful church on the edge of a cliff looking out to sea and, as everyone filed out at the end of the service, they were invited to pick a pebble from the bowl left at the door. The stones had been collected from the beach earlier in the day (with permission) and they were there for the congregation to take in memory of their friend. This offering was given as a reminder that we are all here momentarily and what remains eternal is nature.

Including foraged treasures on our altar, our desk or in our pocket can give us a grounding and connection with Mother Nature. One of my clients went hiking around the Scottish Highlands and brought back a sprig of heather to remind her of the stunning scenery and her happy family holiday, and to give her luck for the winter months ahead. Whatever it may be, keep an eye out for your own charm. It may appear when you least expect it.

∞

SPIRITUAL TOOL: BRINGING THE OUTSIDE IN

- Collect something that calls to you while you are out for a walk. It could be a leaf, a flower, a feather, a shell, sea glass or a pebble. Put it somewhere prominent in your home or keep it in your pocket so you can hold it in your hand when you need the power of the natural world.

- Like the old saying, 'See a penny, pick it up, all the day you will have good luck', I always pick up a penny. I keep hold of it for the day before I give it to someone else so they can share in the luck, and ask them to pass it on to whoever they think needs it.

- I love drying flowers, like daisies, roses and buttercups, by pressing them between books. I then place them on my altar or give them to people I love.

- Sprinkle salt on the altar and draw a pentagram in it as a protective symbol.

- Mistletoe is a mystical plant of festive folklore which signified fertility in pagan culture and it is still a familiar part of our Christmas celebrations. Before you throw your mistletoe out on Twelfth Night, cut a sprig and tuck it away somewhere for the rest of the year to encourage prosperity and love and to give protection.

- Both lavender and rosemary are considered protective herbs which repel negative energy, so I always grow

> lavender at the front of the house and rosemary at the back. I also dry them both and fill little bags to put in my clothes drawers. If you can't grow herbs where you are, then a mirror on the outside of your home will also deflect negativity.

Cold water therapy

This has become a hugely popular activity in recent years and the benefits of wild swimming and cold-water immersion are well documented, with clear rules to be obeyed if you are a beginner. These include choosing recognised and safe areas to enter the water, not going in alone and limiting the time you are submerged, as the beginning of hypothermia can set in before you know it. Check online for detailed advice.

In truth, there are large parts of the country that are nowhere near open water to safely swim in, and if you don't have access to any designated wild swimming locations but you are keen to find out what all the fuss is about, then start in your shower. Begin with the temperature you would normally have and then, thirty seconds before you get out, turn the water to tepid and then cold. Doing this in stages by repeating on a daily basis and steadily increasing the length of time that you spend under the cold water will help build up your stamina, boost your immune system and positively affect your mental health.

A client of mine, Rosie, is evangelical about her sunrise sea swims. She heads down to the beach most mornings to swim with a varied group of people. Often, as they are swimming towards the horizon, watching the day come up, they find it is easier to talk about their problems than when they are on dry land. It can be more comfortable to speak honestly when you do not have to look someone in the eye, and this resonates with me. For those of us who can struggle to open up, this approach also works if you are in a car or out for a walk or jog. If you need to have a difficult conversation with somebody or know they need to do this with you, suggest putting your trainers on and going for a stroll. **Sometimes walking enables talking**. The movement and focus on looking ahead seems to encourage truthful conversation.

As well as getting in water, I like to get on it. I have a paddle board which I love to take to the local reservoir on sunny days and I search out the activity on holiday too. There is something about finding a physical balance that connects me to the spiritual equilibrium I search for in life. It reminds me to live in the moment, focus on the beautiful scenery around me and just enjoy the experience.

The wheel of the year

The wheel of the year plays a big part in my life and directly impacts my wellbeing and decision-making. It has eight significant dates in the Northern Hemisphere. I find the structure deeply reassuring and I match my energy accordingly. If we follow the ancient ebb and flow of the year, we can rest when the earth does and move in accordance with the light.

Winter Solstice – around 21 December – also known as Midwinter, the Hibernal Solstice and Yule, is the shortest day of the year and signals the beginning of the slow return of light. It is a time to write down those things you want to leave behind as the year ends and set fire to them. Clear the decks so you are ready for feasting and festive celebration.

Imbolc – from 1 February through sundown on 2 February – also known as Candlemas, hints at the forthcoming spring. This is a time to emerge from winter hibernation and cleanse and clear any stagnant energy. I always make sure I have several sage sticks for this time of year, when I like to move around the house, wafting the purifying smoke.

Spring Equinox or **Ostara** – around 20 March – is the moment when the light and dark are of similar length. This heralds the full arrival of spring and is a time to set new intentions for the months ahead. I may do this in my journal or as a moon magic spell (see page 104 for details of how to perform this spell).

Beltane or **May Day** – usually celebrated on 1 May – falls halfway between the spring equinox and summer solstice. It marks the beginning of summer and signifies the green growth of living things and the power of fertility and light.

This is a time during which I can begin to feel my messages to the universe are being answered.

Summer Solstice – around 21 June – marks the longest day of the year, meaning the day of the year that has the most hours of sunlight. All hail the sun on this day as we celebrate its divine power and the high point of summer. Use the light to energise and free you. This is a time for motivation and saying, 'I can'.

Lughnasadh or **Lammas** – around 1 August – welcomes the beginning of the harvest season when we recognise plenty and growth. This signifies a new year for me and I use this time as an opportunity to refresh and reassess, encouraging growth in my business and manifesting what I want to bring into my life over the following months.

Autumn Equinox – around 22 September – also known as Mabon, is a moment to give thanks for the harvest and remind us to share our good fortune. This is a good day to think of others, rather than ourselves. As it is about feasting and food, we could donate to a food bank or add some items to the donations point at our local supermarket.

Samhain or **All Hallows'/All Saints' Day** – on 1 November – follows Halloween. It is a time to embrace the spirit world and give blessings to our spiritual people, as this is when the veil between this world and the next is thought to be at its thinnest.

One October, I flew out to Salem in the USA, made famous by the witchcraft trials in 1692. It continues to embrace a mystical culture and I was booked to give readings on Halloween. When I arrived at the venue it was closed, so I wandered around town and popped into a spiritual shop. As I was talking to the owner, I sensed her ex-husband standing next to her, and I told her so. 'He's not dead,' she said. I said maybe I had made a mistake, but I was being told he had died of a heart attack, and she would need to leave tomorrow to sort out his stuff. When I went back to my B&B later that day, the woman called me. I was right: her ex-husband had died, she had to get on a plane, and would I step in while she was gone? I worked there for almost three weeks, giving readings there as well as at the psychic fair and the legendary Halloween ball, which was an amazing experience. I felt like I was home.

Living by the cycle of the moon

I have a deep passion for the moon. Considered a feminine energy and connected to female goddesses, she is my ultimate guiding light, my protector and my source of pure power. Without her I would not be as spiritually open as I am, as she influences my dreams, fires up my intuition, shapes my emotions and speaks to my subconscious. I am led by her mystical 29-day cycle, which represents growth, transformation and renewal.

The sun hitting the moon as viewed from Earth creates eight lunar phases: new moon, waxing crescent, first quarter, waxing gibbous, full moon, waning gibbous, third quarter and waning crescent, and they each carry huge significance. As she impacts me directly, so too does she affect the natural world through light, tides and animal behaviours. She also has a bearing on the balance of our hormones, sleep and even our mental health.

New Moon: Almost in darkness and hard to spot in the night sky, this is the moon of intention and achievement. It heralds a good time for doors to open and dreams to be realised, encouraging fresh starts and new beginnings. I use this moment to tackle something I have been putting off and make a plan for the lunar cycle ahead.

Waxing Crescent: A thin crescent. It takes the baton of growth and intention from the new moon and runs with it. We are ready to lay the foundations for what we have set out to achieve.

First Quarter: Midway between the new and full moon, half the moon shines on the right side. Let's take some action! This is a determined moon, ensuring we manifest those intentions we set out at the beginning of the cycle. This encourages me to make decisions and stick to them.

Waxing Gibbous: Over half of the moon is now lit up from the right side. A persistent yet patient moon. At this point we can adjust any actions, focusing on the details and fine-tuning our goals, knowing the full moon is on its way.

Full Moon: There she is, fully illuminated and spreading her magical light! A thankful moon, this is the time to celebrate what we have achieved. It is also a good time to implant things into the universe, reiterate desires and welcome the physical energy and control that comes with it. Make sure you have your crystals lined up on your windowsill or outside, ready to be cleansed.

Waning Gibbous: As the moon gets smaller on the right side, it begins to embrace the darkness. After the party atmosphere of the full moon, this is a time to take stock, be grateful for what we have achieved and choose what we must release.

Last Quarter: The left-hand side of the moon shines. This is a reflective moon of acceptance and forgiveness, of ourselves and others. It reminds us to be kind and make time for the things that bring us sustenance.

Waning Crescent: Now we have a fingernail crescent moon on the left, the last time we will see the moon before it becomes new again. This waning moon is linked to healing energy, strengthening connections with loved ones and checking our boundaries are in place. It reminds us how important rest and recuperation are. I keep a list at work of people who could use some healing help and I present their names to this moon.

NB: A word here about Mercury in retrograde, the time when Mercury, considered the planet of communication, appears to move in the wrong direction. It is an optical illusion, but the results of these few week cycles, which happen around four times a year, can send us into a tailspin. It is my least favourite time. It's like a bad boyfriend that cheats on you. I find it debilitating, undermining and sneaky, and it creates a spiritual blockage, affecting my entire being. I try to avoid discussing it when it arrives so I can remain as unwelcome as possible, and I call on my inner goddess to give me the strength to surf the negatives and find the positives. Some people say it is a good time to look inward to the heart and make big decisions. I disagree, because from experience there have always been issues in my life around this time, not just with people but with electrical appliances! The lights at work often play up, with one going off as the other one comes on. I always seem to have problems with my phone and recently my fridge broke. Each to their own, but I prefer to sit it out and wait for it to pass.

SPIRITUAL TOOL: MOON MANIFESTATION JOURNAL

Keep a journal of the moon's cycle, writing each of the significant dates down and note what you would like to manifest. Doing this is a helpful way to track your progress through the twenty-nine days and pull you closer to the moon's power. Here are some prompts to help you.

New Moon: What are my intentions for this lunar cycle?

Waxing Crescent: How can I help myself achieve my goals?

First Quarter: Which decisions am I struggling with and how do I action them?

Waxing Gibbous: What do I need to pay closer attention to?

Full Moon: Which of my achievements need more time to manifest?

Waning Gibbous: What have I learned from this lunar cycle?

Last Quarter: What can I let go that no longer serves me?

Waning Crescent: What parts of me need to heal?

Chasing sleep

Good sleep is fundamental to us feeling rested. We know how important it is to our wellbeing, but this doesn't help when we are wide awake at 3am, worrying about our insomnia on top of everything else we may be stressed about. If you find your mind ticking through a myriad of anxieties in the middle of the night, first take a few deep breaths, then imagine a fire crackling away. You want the fire to go out, so don't put more logs on and it will die down much quicker. Now use the same approach for each of your concerns. Over-analysing in the darkness is not going to make them smaller, it will just add more fuel to make them bigger and there will be no benefit to you. Imagine every worry as a small fire and visualise the flames dying out.

There are plenty of other reasons for bad sleep, including lack of exercise, hormones, caffeine, not eating early enough and going to bed too late, but I want to look specifically at the environment in which we sleep, as this may be having a big impact without you realising it. We all need a haven of tranquillity, designed to calm the busy, stressed brain which refuses to switch off.

Take a look around your bedroom. How conducive is it to a peaceful bedtime? Start by taking time to declutter your space, removing any possessions that do not need to be in this room. Think about what you do want to be surrounded by. Things like piles of discarded clothes, boxes of belongings you haven't unpacked, or wardrobes so full the doors won't close, promote a feeling of chaos.

You may need to change your lumpy old mattress or uncomfortable bed, but this may be an expensive undertaking, so you could treat yourself to new bedlinen instead. Wash it regularly, because there is nothing like the smell and feel of fresh sheets, especially if your laundry has dried outside. In the morning, don't forget to make your bed. It changes the look of the room and is so welcoming to come back to at night.

If there is too much light in your room that you can't solve, perhaps from a streetlamp outside, then buy a blackout blind or fabric to line your curtains with. Alternatively, a good eye mask will do the trick and ear plugs help block unwanted sound.

Sleep sprays, scented candles, oils and lotions combining the herbal fragrances of lavender and chamomile can invoke relaxation and ease us gently into the night. So too can a selection of crystals. I have a big bowl of them by my bed, but I select several and put them under my pillow if I need additional help.

If you have a bedside table (and if you don't, I recommend you get one), take everything off it and only return the items you need. This may be a lamp, silent clock, water glass, book, photograph, candle and tissues. Alternatively, arrange your bedside space as an altar.

Ban screens from the bedroom. We know that too much stimulation coupled with the blue light of a screen can disrupt our melatonin levels, which in turn interferes with the circadian rhythm of good sleep. Full disclosure: I love watching TV in bed, but I switch it off at 10pm every night. If you struggle with boundaries and find yourself watching an old film at 2am, then you may need to be stricter with yourself. Try taking the TV out of the bedroom for a couple of weeks and do not bring your phone to bed. I always leave mine in a different room. Knowing that it is next to you means you may reach for it in the middle of the night, and quite soon, a little scrolling becomes a reason to wake up the next night, and then the next. This is how bad habits are formed. Swap your phone alarm for an alarm clock and read an actual book at night rather than on a Kindle. Lastly, do not sleep with a mirror at the end of your bed because it can interfere with the energy in the room and disrupt your sleep. If I'm away from home, I will go so far as to move any mirrors or cover them with a towel.

> **SPIRITUAL TOOL: CRYSTALS FOR SLEEP**
>
> This is my classic combination which I put together to aid better sleep:
>
> **Lapis** for communication
>
> **Blue howlite** to reduce stress
>
> **Clear quartz** for peace
>
> **Purple amethyst** for calm
>
> **Blue sandstone** for relaxation
>
> **Citrine** for intuition
>
> **Green blood stone** for healing
>
> **Black obsidian** to banish nightmares and anxiety

Digital detox

I have already mentioned staying off screens at night, but we also need breaks during the day. We spend so much time on computers, iPads, televisions and phones – they infiltrate every part of our lives. We are drawn to them without realising. Lee will ask Alexa for the current weather forecast and then I ask him why he can't just look out of the window?! I know friends who will pop onto Instagram for what they say will be five minutes, only to look up an hour later. So much of modern interaction is done via screens that we are in danger of losing our social skills, and our time, creativity and personalities are being sucked into these tiny pieces of technology for so little in return. They have become an acceptable addiction. At home, Lee and I have a phone ban at the dinner table, but when I go out to eat, I see diners constantly checking their phones. If we are out with friends, we need to turn our phones off or leave them in our bags and focus our energy on face-to-face communication. So few things are really that urgent, and certainly not notifications from social media.

While we can get a dopamine hit from a message, social media post or consumer scrolling, we can just as easily be distracted, anxious or infuriated by what we may read on our phones. If we put them in a drawer or our bag and leave them, then the issues, just like the good stuff, will be there waiting for us, and we can deal with them on our own terms, rather than being interrupted and bombarded by things we are not ready to see. Checking our messages every five minutes could be changed to checking them every thirty minutes and then every hour. Nothing will have changed, except our brains will no longer be so overstimulated.

As much as I would want to recommend a full digital detox, the reality is that we need screens for work, relaxation, communication, education and our social lives, so it would be hard (and no fun) to eliminate them for long periods of time. What we need to address is how our phones have become our constant companion, more so now that we can pay for things with it. We only need leave the house with that and our keys and we are set for the day. Instead, let's look at a more achievable goal as a starting point. Set some restrictions on your handset around how you access non-urgent apps like social media. Maybe pick a couple of screen-free hours in the week, or make Sunday a phone-free day. Once you get into the routine of this, it is amazing how quickly it becomes a zen zone you want to protect. I believe that holding a piece of electricity in our hand for too long can cause an energy overload, interfering with our own vibrations. **Put it down. Walk away.**

Ritual of recuperation

Rituals are a vital part of our spiritual lives. They ground and reassure us on a daily basis and provide a safe place to return to, carving out the time we need to rest, rethink and re-energise. Rituals can be big occasional activities or small everyday things we do for ourselves, like getting into a scented bath surrounded by candles and then moisturising our bodies (you can learn from my friend Victoria on page 171). I have 'ponytail days' where I tie my hair up, don't put on any make-up and get on with the part of my job that involves making products. I need these days to balance out the ones when I am public facing.

One friend works from home, and she always takes a break mid-morning to scoop ground coffee into a stove pot, place it on the hob, wait for the water to bubble up through the filter and listen to the blip of the coffee as it percolates. She puts out her usual mug and warms the milk in an enamel pan. She moves with care and attentiveness before pouring her coffee and taking it somewhere other than her desk to drink it. I love this idea of a repetitive process that enables the brain to rest, produces the gift of a mug of coffee and allows the space to enjoy it. For all the rushing around, here is something that deserves to take the time it takes and gives the mind a moment to relax in the process. These actions give us permission to pause.

Prioritising physical self-care

I have battled with ill health for most of my life and continue to deal with rheumatoid arthritis, lupus and now the menopause. There are days when they all seem to conspire against me, and I can feel their negative energy attempting to stop me in my tracks. I refuse to let that happen. Like exposing them to the light, I go to see my doctor, meet consultants and try new treatments. The worst thing I could do would be to hide these symptoms away, pretend they are not happening or accept that I will be in pain for the rest of my life. I prioritise my health and I make time for these appointments. If you have been worried about a health issue but have not had time to go to your GP or would prefer to bury your head in the sand, I would urge you to get checked out. **We owe it to ourselves to be as physically healthy as we can be**, so along with good sleep and regular exercise, we need to pay attention to our body, its aches and pains and the messages it could be sending us that all is not well. Ignoring this will speed our slide into burnout and our desperation for rest.

SPIRITUAL TOOL: ESSENTIAL OILS

If I wasn't a psychic, I would be a perfumier. I can't think of anything nicer than playing around with delicious scents and creating mind-blowing combinations. From the early days of my career, I have worked with essential oils, and it is not only something I love, but it instantly transports me to a calm and sacred space. Below is a list of my favourite pairings which not only smell divine, but give intention to your day. Try a few drops in an oil burner, added to olive or argan oil and rubbed over your body, or turned into a body scrub with sea salt.

Vetiver and ylang ylang: For affirmation – 'My mind is clear and focused'

Citrus and rosemary: To relax and de-stress – 'I have found my inner peace'

Geranium and orange: To enhance moon magic – 'I call upon the magic of the moon to make my wishes and dreams come true'; 'I am protected and safe'

> **Chamomile and lavender:** For good sleep – 'I am relaxed and ready to sleep'
>
> **Sandalwood and black pepper:** For power – 'I am strong, focused and in control'
>
> **Patchouli and lavender:** To balance the chakras – 'My chakras are balanced and moving freely'
>
> **Orange and lavender:** For healing – 'I am healthy, calm and relaxed'
>
> **Orange and spearmint:** For spirituality – 'I am connected to my spirit guides and guardian angels'

Do not run away from yourself

As you know, I am very good at only accepting invitations for things I want to do, and this goes some way to preserving my social battery, but I can still get caught out if several dates come along at once. I know FOMO (fear of missing out) is a modern phenomenon, exacerbated by social media posts showing you things you weren't invited to, but how about JOMO (joy of missing out)?! We need to embrace this. As we are on a mission to bring more rest and recuperation into our lives, let's turn the negative of not doing something into the positive of protecting our energy.

What I am also saying is: do not run away from yourself. Sarah, a client of mine, was going through a terrible divorce and was filling her time by going on dating websites and meeting men. This became a pattern she couldn't seem to break. She realised that in the course of a month she had not been alone for a single minute because she was either with her children or her friends, or drinking in bars with potential suitors. It took a health scare for her to finally take stock and listen to those of us around her who were urging her to take a break. She was not going to begin to heal and move on from her broken marriage until she could sit on the sofa alone in the evening and be happy in her own company.

SPIRITUAL TOOL: MERIDIANS AND PULSE POINTS

One of the quickest, easiest and most subtle ways to relieve stress or reconnect with yourself is to stimulate one of the pressure points around the body, either targeting the meridians or applying essential oils to our pulse points.

I will often rub my left palm with the thumb of my right hand, using a soothing circular motion, or take the skin between the thumb and forefinger and apply pressure gently for a minute or so. I also have a palm stone of fluorite which helps with concentration, and I rub my thumb on it to relax and focus on me. When I am feeling nervous, I tap on my temples to regulate my system and distract myself. These small but meaningful exercises link to our meridians around the body.

> The meridian pathway, the foundation of Chinese alternative medicine, is believed to carry electric energy around our system. There are twelve main meridians, including the five yin (heart, spleen, lungs, kidneys, liver) and the five yang (small intestine, large intestine, stomach, urinary bladder, gallbladder), which can be externally navigated by around 400 points that are used in acupuncture, tapping and applying pressure.
>
> As philosophical as the meridians may be considered, pulse points are physical places where we can locate a pulse. We feel them in our head, neck, elbow, wrist, groin, knee, ankle and foot, and they indicate where the blood is closest to the surface of the skin. These are the best points to apply essential oils for rapid absorption, ideally to a spot where you will benefit from the relaxing scent, like the wrist or neck.

The pursuit of creativity

The idea of a 'hobby' may be just as antiquated as talking about what we do in our 'spare time', but this is another concept I want to campaign for, particularly when it is in pursuit of creativity. Whether it involves picking up a paintbrush, taking a pottery class, writing, journalling, knitting, sewing or crafting, there are so many stimulating ways to find an antidote to a frenetic lifestyle. Pick up a hobby you may have let lapse or try something you have never done before. There is something so wonderfully meditative and absorbing in artistic endeavours, letting our industrious hands distract our brain and focusing only on the task in front of us. Now, there's a way to stay off screens.

One of the quickest ways to escape the real world for a while is to disappear into a book. It could be a sweeping literary classic, a modern romantic comedy or an epic sci-fi fantasy, or you may prefer non-fiction. The words of people who you respect and value, and who may have a keener, sharper, more articulate view on the world than others, can really help. They can sum up a feeling or a thought we may have been trying to unscramble for a very long time. Take time to read, whether it is books or articles, and gravitate to those writers you would want to sit next to at dinner. As I am dyslexic and have a commute to work, I veer towards a good audiobook or podcast, and I also look for powerful quotes and affirmations that reinforce my strength and belief in myself. I write them in my journal or stick them next to my desk for easy reference.

When I need a balm for my soul, I turn to one of my favourite pastimes, which admittedly also ties into my work, but feeds my inspiration and excitement in equal measure. I get brewing with oils, using my intuition and judgement to put together a combination of scents to create unique fragrances. Smell is hugely important to me. It triggers my senses, reflects the past and transports me to a safe and happy place. If I need to build emotional strength, I turn to my potions and spend a couple of absorbing hours making up recipes. If any of them turn into

Psychic Sisters products, I try to keep notes, because I go on my gut instinct and then find it hard to repeat. Everything we sell is handmade and occasionally I will personalise something. We had an order from a customer I had never met and as we blended the oil, I added an extra shot of lavender because I felt she required something stronger to help her deflect negative energy. She will not have known I did that, but I sensed her need and answered it.

Live in the moment

I almost didn't include a section about choosing to live in the moment because it's so obvious. However, as much as we hear the phrase 'live in the moment' repeated across popular culture and social media, I think it has become white noise and we are in danger of ignoring the message. It is now a bit of a cliché. Maybe it is time to liberate this phrase or use a different one that means the same thing. Perhaps 'be present' works better. The point is that while we may think we are getting better at living in the moment, there will be everyday examples of us finding this difficult to do. It is not how modern life is set up, particularly when we have a mobile phone in one hand and a drive to move faster through our lives. Take the time to slow down.

THE ENERGY OF GREEN

Crystal: Green aventurine is a healing stone, thought to be one of the luckiest. This beautiful quartzite represents nature and helps to alleviate anxiety and stress. It evokes balance, wellbeing, renewal and growth and brings stability to the heart.

Colour: Immerse yourself in green or try the Japanese art of forest bathing, wander through nature paying close attention, or sit silently. Put a plant on your desk or by your bed and care for it daily. Water it, talk to it, move it to sunlight. Paint a wall in your home green.

Affirmation:

I have a calm mind, body and soul.

Journal Prompt: What are some of the ways I can think of to help me unwind?

Step 7

FINDING YOUR SELF

Self-care	Self-esteem	Self-awareness
Self-compassion	Self-worth	Self-acceptance
Self-confidence	Self-belief	Self-respect

How many of these do you practise? While they are different from each other, they all equal the same thing:

Self-love

As Whitney Houston sang, we find the greatest love of all inside us, but it isn't quite as easy to achieve as the song makes out. It's a slippery, elusive, tenuous creature that we may catch hold of for a moment before it is scared off by our frustrations, doubts and lack of self-esteem. I am not suggesting that we should live in a continual state of self-love – I know I don't – but neither must we lose sight of it. We need to know how to summon it at any point, no matter what is happening in our lives.

I have been leading you towards self-love by tackling your confidence, intuition and boundaries through spiritual tasks. I have shown you how to tap into your potential, revealed the route to your inner goddess and considered how to rest and recharge. Now we are at the penultimate point in our quest to live a more intentional life and, with the help of what we have already covered, it is within your grasp. Remember what you already know. The work you have done will stand you in good stead for this final act of self-love.

I wouldn't be surprised if you find this the hardest chapter to connect with. I think there can be a lot of embarrassment around the idea of loving ourselves. We are used to showing kindness, compassion, care and respect to other people, but when we try to direct this inwards, it can feel uncomfortable and insincere. Perhaps we do not feel worthy or able to receive this sort of self-declaration (yet another 'self'), but until we do, we will not gain the depth of fulfilment we desire. **Let's find the person we want to be rather than the person everyone perceives we are.** This is not to say that once we have transcended to that level of enlightenment, we will never leave it. It is an ongoing mission.

I can still recall the depth of self-loathing I had as a teenager, like many of us going through adolescence, and now, as an adult who knows better, I find myself slipping backwards occasionally. Maybe because I am too busy, tired or stressed to take any notice of who I am and what I want. When this happens, I force myself to slow down, recognise that my energy has shifted and take a step back from everything. As soon as I turn my attention inwards with honesty and love and look to my centre, I begin to stabilise and feel balance returning.

Save yourself

Nobody is coming to save you. This phrase often pops up in the media and it always makes me stop and think. On the face of it, it may sound like a harsh statement, making us feel as if we are in the middle of an apocalypse and facing a train load of zombies. It seems desolate and depressing, but in essence it is true, and I want to turn it into a positive affirmation. **As supported and loved as we may be by family and friends, our life is in our hands.** This is down to us. We cannot and should not hand this responsibility to somebody else and rely on them for our happiness. While others can support, inspire and encourage our search for self-love, they can't achieve it for us. We either feel it or we don't.

The same is true of hanging our hopes on a particular situation or achievement. Until we find peace within ourselves and gain strength from our internal being rather than external influences, we will not find fulfilment.

Can you pinpoint issues that are stopping you from gaining contentment? Sometimes there are situations that have to change to enable you to be happy with who you are. Let's look at areas where you may need to save yourself.

- Are you stagnating in a relationship you cannot get out of? Why is this proving hard to extricate yourself from?

Are you worried about hurting the other person? Do you have money issues or not want to be alone? Is this a partnership that leads you away from self-love? Do you feel undermined, unsupported and taken for granted? Have you been consumed by being part of a couple and forgotten who you are in the process?

- Are you struggling in your professional life? Is this the job you wanted? Is the work environment healthy and respectful? Do you get on with your colleagues or do you feel like a fish out of water? Have you found yourself caught in a career you do not want?

- Is your home life safe, happy and restorative? Are you living in the area and community you want to be part of? Do you wish you could move and live somewhere completely different?

- Are you saddled with a big debt? Do you show a lack of control around financial issues? Are you living beyond your means?

- Do you say yes to things when you really mean no?

- Is it hard to get away from the Negative Nellies in your life?

- Are you seeking change but don't know where to start?

I can't answer these questions for you; only you can do that. As many as I have written here, there are countless more questions I could be asking. Imagine I am gently poking you with a stick, waking you from autopilot and turning you to face the root cause of your problem. This is an opportunity for you to interrogate yourself about how much of your life reflects true happiness and what percentage is fear, anxiety and exhaustion. What is it you could change if you were completely free to do so? Or, more to the point, **what is it you need to save yourself from?**

I have a good friend, Victoria, who was in an abusive professional relationship before I met her. This happened at her workplace, a department store she loved, for a make-up brand she enjoyed being part of, with colleagues who were friends. So far, so perfect. All apart from one workmate, who systematically bullied her for six years. Every evening, Victoria would check the rota for the following day to see if she had to work with the bully and, if she did, she had to psych herself up, strap on her mental armour and get through the shift as best she could.

One morning, ready for the onslaught, Victoria arrived at work to find this colleague was not there. After putting up her protective forcefield to enable her to survive, the relief she felt at not needing it was overwhelming. So overwhelming in fact that she burst into tears. Her surprising reaction reflected years of subtle, invasive abuse, and she couldn't stop sobbing. She felt as if she had broken into a thousand pieces. Why had she not faced this issue before now? How was it that a seemingly insignificant moment of brief reprieve caused such a flood of emotion? This was significant enough to be a catalyst in what Victoria did next. She handed in her notice the same day. Her CEO couldn't believe it and didn't want to lose her from the cosmetics company, so the company arranged for a transfer to a different department store.

The experience of deep anguish had instigated a lightbulb moment where Victoria could see exactly what she had been forced to accept for years and how she no longer needed to deal with it. She let go of what she couldn't control and focused on what she could, as she hung on to the insightful shift in energy. She realised that the ninety-nine reasons she always gave for staying in her job were not as important as the one reason why she had to leave. She knew she couldn't remain in a work environment that continued to compromise her self-worth and happiness. It was at this point, she now says, that she knew she loved herself. This was the catalyst for change. After six years of miserably managing a difficult situation, she was prepared to walk away from her job with nothing to go on to. She saved herself. This is an inspiring story, although I wish Victoria could have had this epiphany earlier and I hope this inspires you to action if you are similarly stuck.

I see this a lot with clients asking about their relationships, particularly if they are having an extra-marital affair. The big question is always: will the other person leave their partner? I find these readings take a lot of energy because invariably the answer is no, they will not leave, but the client doesn't want to hear that. One client, Alice, was convinced her lover would leave his wife and when I told her they were going to have another baby, she refused to believe me and became very angry. I didn't charge her for the session, and I didn't expect her to ever return. Six months later, Alice turned up to see me and said she wanted to pay for the previous reading because what

I had told her turned out to be true. Her lover's wife had just given birth to their second child. The sad truth was that Alice didn't walk away until he had a third child. Thankfully she is now happily married to a lovely guy who adores her.

SPIRITUAL TOOL: CHAKRA HEALING

Working through our chakras is a brilliant way of clearing blockages, letting go of stagnated energy and cleansing us of negativity. This is one of the exercises I use on a regular basis.

Take a nice deep inhale and, as you do, visualise a bright white light coming towards you. As you slowly exhale, send away the negative stress on the outward breath. Now feel the light come in through the **crown** chakra on the top of your head and picture a tight bud which opens into a beautiful pink flower and spins like a vortex, spreading energy to the **third eye**, between your eyebrows. Now the bud turns into a purple flower and whirls around, sending power to the **throat** chakra, whose bud becomes a blue flower. Moving down to the **heart** chakra, the bud blossoms into a green flower, which spins and sends vibrations to the **solar plexus** chakra in the stomach, where the bud reveals a yellow flower. Breathe the energy down to the orange flower of the **sacral** chakra, just below the navel, and then to the **root** chakra at the base of the spine and the bud opens to reveal a red flower. Now, visualise the beautiful colours merging into a breathtaking rainbow and push this energy back up your body to your crown chakra and down to your root chakra. As you do, feel it flowing through all your chakras, opening, cleansing and clearing them as the vibrations move freely. Once you are back at your root chakra, do the process in reverse, travelling to each chakra – sacral, solar plexus, heart, throat, third eye and then crown – as each flower folds back into a bud. Visualise yourself closing each chakra until you get to the crown. Finally, imagine a cloak of protection around you and move forward freely into the rest of your day.

Find the positives to the negatives

To echo what I have said before, nothing beats negativity more than embracing all the factors that create it. Failure? Do your worst. Rejection? You don't scare me. Crisis? I am strong enough to withstand you. I am not suggesting you seek them out and put yourself in places to experience them to prove a point or test yourself; this is about taking the power away from those feelings. If we can reduce their impact in our minds and shush the negative voice inside us, we can face the fears with a different mindset. **Remember, everything happens for a**

reason, and learning from the bad stuff can catapult us somewhere infinitely better. Just look at Victoria.

I know we can't be positive all the time, but we do need to raise our optimism regularly to avoid spiralling into a gloomy mindset. Thinking black thoughts can create a self-fulfilling prophecy, so displaying a positive mental attitude, even when we are not particularly feeling it, promotes a much-needed upbeat outlook and general wellbeing. It may fall into the 'fake it till you make it' category, but this is not disingenuous, nor am I suggesting we pretend everything is okay in front of others. We can be honest about the tough times and show an emotional response to it, but we can also boost our positivity when we need to. This is about repositioning our brain patterns and sending our thoughts down sunnier pathways. If we do this regularly, then our brain begins to choose that option of its own accord.

A good way to start is to be alert to your next negative thought or experience and respond to it positively. Let's say your car breaks down and you have to wait for a recovery vehicle. Firstly, the psychic in me would believe this has saved you from a bad accident and your spirit guide has stepped in to give you a puncture or engine trouble to protect you from a worse fate. Secondly, I would also see this as bonus time. While you are waiting, you can sit in the car and meditate, write a list of things you want to achieve over the coming weeks or contact people you need to catch up with. Sometimes being stuck for a while (physically and emotionally) makes us creative and, yes, we may miss out on wherever our car was supposed to be taking us, but if we handle it correctly, we could gain too.

I also want you to take this approach with people. If you have a Negative Nelly in your life, then they are likely to be bringing you down, as well as themselves. Take a break from them or slip away altogether if you can. I have mentioned this before, but the particular sort of energy they bring is the type to suck the lifeblood from you and leave you husklike before they slope off to their next victim. They won't even realise they are doing it, but you will, so practise your boundary-setting and extricate yourself as kindly you can.

Victoria has come a long way since those tough days at the hands of an unkind colleague. She knows she will not repeat that situation again, but it doesn't mean she has found the meaning of life and can skip through the daisies for the rest of her days. She still doubts herself, finds some days harder than others, battles low self-esteem and carries the scars of her experience. In addition, she struggles with her weight and has to fight the complicated feelings she has towards this. While she is more positive than she is negative, she has to work on it every day and finds small yet significant ways to keep herself on track. One of these is through smell. She has several jars of beautifully fragranced body lotions and every day she will slather one on after her morning shower. This has become an important daily ritual, and as she moisturises her skin and breathes in the luxurious scent of whichever one she is drawn to, she says to herself, 'Today you are okay and today you are enough.' Pampering her body like this gives it a direct message that she will take care of it and love herself, no matter what her shape and size.

SPIRITUAL TOOL: PAMPER DIY

As I have mentioned before, I surround myself with beautiful smells. Whether it is at home, at work, in my car or on my body, scent is an integral part of my day and a tool to keep me calm, focused and happy. It can summon up happy memories or instantly transport me to somewhere familiar and safe. Sometimes I will subconsciously choose an essential oil before realising I am drawn to it because I may be looking for protection, relaxation or energy. Blending my own uniquely personal combinations becomes a meditation in itself – as does making my own beauty products.

I often go into the kitchen, pour a drop of olive oil into the palm of my hand and add a couple of drops of essential oil (never use herbal oils directly on the skin and check they are dermatologically friendly) before combining them. I highly recommend rubbing the liquid into your arms, base of your neck and hands and relishing the wafts of beautiful scent that surround you for the next few hours.

1. First, choose your oils. If I want a calming, sleep-inducing experience, I will use lavender or chamomile. If I want an energising bath, I may add a couple of drops of eucalyptus, and to diffuse stress I go for clary sage. (For more inspiration, see the combinations on page 155.)

2. Once you have filled your bath with warm (not too hot) water, add a generous scoop of Epsom salts, followed by a few drops of oil, and disperse into the water with your hands, giving everything a good mix around.

3. Now scatter some dried herbs over the water (I use lavender and rosemary) and light a few candles. Make sure you have a fluffy, clean towel nearby before sinking into the experience.

Are you your own worst enemy?

Let's talk about another 'self' – the ability to self-sabotage. Our own destructiveness can stand in the way of us reaching the very centre of who we are and achieving balance in our lives. We all have a tendency towards self-destruction, whether it is as small as staying up too late or as big as dealing with addiction. Sometimes it is hard to find the motivation to move our day or our choices in the right direction. We vow to take control, but we do little to make this happen. Instead, we watch others and assume their lives are so much better than our own. Like the swans that glide across the pond near where I live, our outward serenity often belies the fact that our feet are paddling frenetically under the water.

Switch off the inner critic who likes to launch brutal attacks and let this commentary be drowned out by a kind and compassionate voice who can empathetically evaluate a situation. This is a big step towards self-love and away from self-hate and judgement. Be ready to repel every negative ball of energy, batting it back with the full force of your racket of positivity.

This also goes for comparing ourselves to others, which is a fool's game and achieves nothing. Like running in a race, do not look behind you, nor to your left or right to where your competitors might be. Instead, just stare straight ahead and focus on the outcome you want. **What does it matter what other people are doing? It is you that counts**. We have all wished to be someone else at some point in our lives, but what is it specifically about them that we are envious of? Their house? Their car? Their career success? Their happy relationship? These are all things we can achieve for ourselves, if we are happy, confident and appreciative of who we are. And you know what? We may find that the possession we lusted after isn't what we actually want and the person we admired has their own set of problems to contend with.

Fall in love with yourself before you fall in love with anyone else

One of the most frequently asked questions from clients during a reading is about their romantic relationships, either whether they will find 'the one' or if they are with the right person.

Many people place this higher on their priority list than finding love with themselves. I understand; I have been there. I know how it feels to believe that being loved by someone validates us in some way and makes us worthy of attention. We are not settled in ourselves until we have found someone to settle with, but that is not a good foundation for a relationship. **Needing something and wanting it are two very different things, and our soulmate is more likely to arrive at the point when we stop looking.**

A client of mine, Danielle, had sworn off relationships after eight years of being caught in unsuitable trysts that went nowhere. She had tried taking a break in the past but had always been seduced by the next possibility that came along. After another brief dalliance, she decided enough was enough. She was adamant that she was stepping back from the dating scene, and she had no interest in pursuing any liaison. After a couple of months, she felt happier than she had in a long time; she was looking after her physical, mental and spiritual health and relishing her power returning. Her energy was focused inwards and, in return, it shone out of her like a beacon of contentment. A chance meeting with an old friend, who was also on a break from futile relationships, sparked something. The timing, their shared mindset and the strength they held as single people was key, and they fell in love. I won't say they lived happily ever after, because nothing is ever that simple, but they are still together.

For those of us who are in a romantic couple, but are questioning whether it is right or not, we must ask ourselves what our motivation is for staying. Are we scared of being alone? Are we repeating destructive patterns of previous relationships, or stuck in the 'on and off' of a boomerang tryst? Are we always attracted to the wrong person? Have we allowed ourselves to be consumed by our partner? We also have to be realistic about what relationships really entail. They will be boring at times, there will have to be compromise, disagreements, fundamental differences of opinion and the general ebb and flow of emotions. We have to separate the truth of a healthy partnership from the lies of a toxic one, and that is much harder to do if we don't show love for ourselves. You wouldn't put someone you love in a difficult situation, so don't put yourself in one. Protect yourself as much as you would those you are close to.

SPIRITUAL TOOL: SELF-LOVE MANIFESTATION

I use this practice to manifest and connect to every aspect of 'self', keeping present and engaged. It's a brilliant one to turn to when you need to shake yourself out of complacency and set your challenge for the week. Using astrology as a guide, each day will attract something different.

Monday: Governed by the moon, this is a day for **healing** and an opportunity to take stock before the week picks up pace. Do not start anything big or do too much; instead, focus on positive intentions for the week ahead. Mondays get such a bad press, and it can feel like we are walking through treacle after the weekend, so it is not a day to put ourselves under pressure.

Mantra for the day: I am healed and ready for the week.

Ritual for the day: Write down your goals for the week ahead.

Tuesday: Governed by Mars, this is a day for **power** and **strength**, a time to forge ahead and make changes.

Mantra for the day: I am strong, focused and positive.

Ritual for the day: Take Victoria's tip of using your favourite body oil or lotion, and as you rub it into your skin, breathe in energy with the scent and repeat your mantra for the day.

Wednesday: Governed by Mercury, the planet of communication, this day is also connected to **financial abundance** and **intelligence**.

Mantra for the day: I am generating financial stability.

Ritual for the day: Give something back, e.g. donate something to the food bank in the local supermarket.

Thursday: Governed by Jupiter, this day is the best for **intuition** and **spiritual awareness**.

Mantra for the day: I am connected to my spirit guides and guardian angels.

Ritual for the day: Look for symbols and signs, a feather, a robin, a message from above.

Friday: Governed by Venus, the planet of **love**, this is the day for romantic assignations, friendships, socialising and loving ourselves.
Mantra for the day: I am loved and happy.
Ritual for the day: Treat yourself and spoil someone close to you. It could be buying you both a coffee.

Saturday: Governed by Saturn, this day represents **boundaries** and **self-discipline**.
Mantra for the day: I am in control of my boundaries.
Ritual for the day: Do not feel obliged to say yes to everything; say 'no' at least once today.

Sunday: Governed by the sun, it is a day for the **Divine Self.**
Mantra for the day: I am content within myself.
Ritual for the day: Have a pamper bath, take time out for you and find your yoga (see page 22).

Pain is growth

Being in emotional pain following any sort of loss, whether it is a relationship break-up, a job we loved or the unbearable death of someone close to us, can cause our self-love to shrivel as we are overwhelmed by sorrow. There is a process to this sort of agony and, if we allow our grief to carve out its own truthful course, we are more likely to reignite our love for ourselves in time. In amongst all the heartfelt advice, someone may urge us to 'let it go', as if our pain is a balloon we are holding on to and by releasing the string it will float away into the clouds, never to be seen again. I don't know about you, but I find that a hard concept to grasp. Letting something go implies it will instantly disappear, and that isn't possible with certain types of pain. **Instead, I say 'let it be'**. It exists, we respectfully acknowledge it, we allow it to stay as long as it doesn't continually remind us it is there, and it takes the pressure off moving through a grieving journey that we should take at our own speed. As a spiritualist, I do not fear the death of loved ones. I know that this is an unusual attitude, but I have the comfort of their energy telling me they are safe and well, and believing it is merely a transition of the soul.

I would like to say something here about 'getting closure'. As much as we may need this at certain points, we are usually asking for this from others, and they may not be prepared or able to give it. And even if they do, will it be enough to satisfy us and help us move on? Instead of focusing on this, we can channel our own energy into building self-love, so we no longer need the validation of others. This is not about forgiveness or answers from others, it's about accepting and healing ourselves. Being beholden to someone else for resolution is a dangerous place to be, but being beholden to ourselves to let things be and move on is the best form of closure there is.

Be your own psychic

By following the steps in this book, this is exactly where you are heading. Embracing a more magical approach, practising spiritual exercises and allowing our beliefs to stretch beyond this realm opens doors to places inside us we never knew existed. All the tips I include are designed to give a deeper sense of who we are and support our desires for a life of purpose and contentment. How far you want to delve is up to you, but injecting a little spirituality into your life can change your outlook, your decision-making and, ultimately, your future. Have faith in the unexplained and give yourself permission to be open to this and to investigate further. This may be the start of a new understanding.

Be kind to yourself

A new client, Tara, reminded me recently of how crucial self-care is. She will regularly arrange an Appreciation Day for herself, and this time she visited me in Selfridges for a reading and then went off to treat herself to a doughnut and a browse of the store. It was such a simple act of self-love, and my Psychic Sisters and I discussed it at length, considering what we would treat ourselves to, if only we had more time. And that is the point. None of us feel like we have time to 'waste' on spoiling ourselves when we have partners, children, friends, work, bills to pay and chores to do. There is always an excuse about why we can't do something, but what if we took a day off to be with ourselves? No distractions from others or compromise around what they may want to do, just a whole day of self-awareness; to please ourselves, eat what we want, do what we want to do. And it has to be guilt-free, otherwise it defeats the object. Getting to know ourselves by doing something nice is much more fun than realisations we gain as we battle with something uncomfortable. There are lessons to learn in everything, and sometimes, just because it seems like fun, doesn't mean it won't help us grow.

SPIRITUAL TOOL: FIRE CEREMONY

A fire ceremony is a universal practice that can help in so many situations, but I think it is most powerful when it is focused on our deepest desires.

As part of ancient tradition in many cultures, fire represents the death of the old life and the rebirth of the new, like a phoenix rising from the ashes. It is an integral part of the cleansing and healing process, whether outdoors in the natural world, inside in the home environment or in a burning bowl. It affords us warmth, comfort and reflection and creates a meditative moment as we watch the flames in companionable peace, carrying additional significance at both the summer and winter solstices as well as at New Year.

Utilising fire is not just for those times, but for whenever you want to give thanks or clear negative energy, and can be part of a group event or a solitary practice. Bringing something for the fire can either be a gift of manifestation or an act of resolution.

A Manifestation Ritual: If you want to manifest, then add a piece of wood or herb to your fire, chosen with their meaning in mind. I take the symbolism from a combination of folklore and paganism. For example, it is thought that the apple tree symbolises health, happiness and immortality, while the ash represents peace, wisdom and empowerment. Turn to the beech for integrity and truth, the birch for rebirth, and the eucalyptus for clearing negative energy. The fir means strength, the sacred hawthorn symbolises love, holly is for fertility and ivy for fidelity. Pine is for purity. Herbs have similar significance, and I use rosemary for remembrance, chamomile for calm, lavender for reassurance and protection and sage for cleansing negative energy and engendering wisdom. Watch the wood burn and direct your thoughts to the action you want to provoke. You can even speak aloud your wishes and describe what you want to happen.

A Resolution Ritual: Call upon the transformative power of the flames to cleanse negativity and release what you no longer need. Take a piece of paper and write down what may be troubling you, whether it is an issue with someone close, a money worry or an internal struggle with yourself. Note down as much as you want to say, using the opportunity to write your thoughts as a cathartic experience. You may have several issues to face. Write each on a separate piece of paper. Now read it aloud if you are alone, or in your head if you are with others, and then give it to the fire. Watch the smoke rise and the concern turn to ash. Repeat until you have burned each piece of paper. Sit watching the flames and repeat the affirmation, 'Let it go, let it be.' (You'll find a Gratitude Ritual incorporating this approach on page 195.)

Practise acceptance

True acceptance of who we are is hard won. Sometimes we have to pretend to accept ourselves and difficult situations, maybe even force the feeling of acceptance regularly until we find it easier to access. There are times when things are simply out of our control. Accepting them for what they are can diffuse the stress, fear and emotion around them. I know this is easy to say and difficult to do, but there is such liberation in letting expectations go. I am thinking of situations ranging from the intensely personal, like a relationship break-up or illness to the domestically mundane like the washing machine malfunctioning with your favourite pair of jeans inside. There will be resolution, in one way or another, but first we have to accept the position we find ourselves in rather than rail against it. Only then can we find an answer or a way to live within the restrictions it presents.

THE ENERGY OF ORANGE

Crystal: Carnelian, a stunning orange stone which is linked to creativity and the heart's desire. It is the stone of vision and courage and enables you to look to your centre.

Colour: Wearing a splash of orange can connect you or, if that particular colour isn't your thing, try carrying an orange object about you.

Affirmation: *I love myself.*

Journal Prompt: What do I love about myself? What would I organise on my own Appreciation Day?

Step 8

HOW TO BE GRATEFUL

As this chapter is about practising gratitude, let me start by thanking you for picking up this book and putting your trust in me to lead you to a more intentional life. We have climbed up seven purposeful levels, culminating in this, the eighth; eight is a magical number of infinity, harmony and balance – concepts which have echoed throughout our quest.

I count my blessings every single day. I think this is an integral part of acknowledging the good and bad of life and it can be the fastest way to find the positives in a tricky situation. Rather than complaining about what we *don't* have, let's think about what we *do* have and be thankful for it. This displays a strength of character which, like a muscle, needs regular exercise to maintain it. Whenever we feel stuck and stagnant and need a sharp shift in our perspective, being reminded of what is already ours is a good mental trick to disperse negativity.

Over sixteen years ago, I was booked to do a photoshoot as part of my regular column in *Spirit & Destiny* magazine.

A friend lived in an old stately home which had been divided into apartments and she offered me the place as a venue for the shoot. I hadn't been there before, but I thought the backdrop sounded ideal for what we wanted, so I gratefully accepted the invitation and turned up on the day with the photographer and stylists. Everything that could go wrong did, including the fire alarm going off and the fire engines being called out. It was an absolute disaster, and the resulting photographs echoed this, but, in the midst of the chaos, I turned to one of the team and said I was going to live there. I knew I had found my home, even though my introduction to it was chaotic and it was financially out of my reach at the time. Years later, I moved into a lovely cottage in the grounds of the big house with swans on the lake and horses in the fields, and not a single day goes by when I don't express my eternal gratitude for finding my life here.

Being grateful is a powerful state and creates a positive response in others, not just ourselves, spreading warmth and wellbeing. It feels good to be appreciated and to appreciate in return. Saying a simple 'thank you' with sincerity and a smile goes a long way, and there is often no need to do anything further. However, sometimes it is important to show gratitude through action as well as words by writing a card, making someone a coffee, buying flowers or finding other small ways to highlight our thanks and give the receiver a surprising and heart-warming moment in their day. Who wouldn't want that?! We can also show our gratitude for the life we lead with a selfless act like volunteering for a charitable cause or helping within our local community.

There is always someone worse off than ourselves, but we have to be careful not to use that as a ruler against which we measure our own luck. This feels too close to schadenfreude to me, the voyeuristic ogling of others' misfortune in order to make us feel better about our own lives. There is a fine line between being relieved and being grateful, and sometimes comparison to others crosses into a place none of us want to be. I think the answer lies in positioning our thanks with a more holistic attitude, rather than focusing on a local or global tragedy and being grateful it isn't happening to us.

It is important to have a grateful heart and soul, and not just go through the motions or summon it for ulterior motives. We must truly believe that we are blessed and thankful for the world around us, who we are as people, our physical capabilities and the wondrous miracle of life. Here we are! Some of us more battered, bruised and broken than others, but look: we survive and we can thrive.

Gratitude is good for us.

Being thankful in the everyday

Whether it is to someone who brought you coffee in a café, the person who held the door open for you, a colleague who helped you with a work issue or your partner for cooking dinner, say thank you. **Show people you appreciate them.** Sometimes we are so distracted by our own worlds, we forget to appreciate the small gestures and moments of kindness we are shown. We can also be inclined to say this more to strangers than we do to our own family and friends because of overfamiliarity and expectation. Then there are those times when thanking someone is incredibly difficult because it is the acknowledgement of something uncomfortable or embarrassing. Shame can make us lose our manners. Like the couple I read about who were cut off by the tide, stranded on the rocks and then rescued by the RNLI. They were so mortified that when they reached the safety of shore, they got out of the boat and marched off without a word of thanks to their saviours.

As well as thanking people, look for those moments or the little things you can be grateful for. A hot mug of tea when you wake up, finding a fiver in your pocket, being absorbed in a good book, the slugs not eating the runner beans, finding a parking space when you are in a rush or hearing an owl as you get into bed. I could fill an entire book with things to be thankful for. Don't be afraid to share your gratitude out loud to the universe. 'Thank you, parking angel, for directing me to this space and for reducing my levels of stress!'

My cold-water swimming friend, Rosie, thanks the sea every time she wades out of it. She turns to face the horizon and gives her appreciation for a safe and restorative swim, accepting her insignificance in the face of the magnificence of the natural world.

∞

SPIRITUAL TOOL: GRATITUDE MEDITATION

1. Find a comfortable place to sit or lie down, preferably with your eyes closed to enable you to look inward.

2. Activate your meditation breath, with deep inhales through your nose and slow, audible exhales through your mouth.

3. Spend a few moments relaxing into this state of being, aware of your breathing and your physical body.

4. Now imagine a feeling of gratitude travelling through your body like a warm pink light, cleansing you of negativity and filling you with thanks.

5. Visualise the people you are thankful for and call them to your mind's eye; your parents, your partner, your children, other significant members of your family, your friends or colleagues. Let go of any irritations that may come up as you go through this process. Bow your head in appreciation of each person and thank them for who they are and what they mean to you.

6. Picture your surroundings. In your mind, focus in on the room you are sitting in and then slowly zoom out to see your home, your street, your town, your country and then into the atmosphere where you

can look back at our beautiful Mother Earth. Think of things you are grateful for in the natural world; air, water, plants. Now slowly return to our planet, to your country, your town, your street and your home until you are firmly back in the centre of your being.

7. Turn inwards to yourself. Show gratitude for all you are – your physical body, your mental health, your creativity, your spirituality. Bow your head in deep thanks to yourself.

8. At the closing of your meditation, visualise the pink light moving through your body and think who you would choose to send it to after its service to you. You can either visualise this happening or send the person a message of thanks after your practice.

9. Take time to open your eyes, stretch and step back into your day, feeling the benefits of this mediation of appreciation.

Keep a journal of gratitude

As you will now gather, I am a big fan of noting things down, whether it is lists, spiritual exercises, affirmations, doodles or journalling. I find it a great way of working out what I really think about something and connecting different parts of me, as my subconscious or my spirit guides speak through the pen. I also enjoy jotting down things I am grateful for before I go to sleep. It is a good way to assess the day, think about the positives and negatives and highlight the elements I want to show thanks for. Establishing this as a morning or evening practice is a practical way to really underline our blessings and pay homage to them. Making it a regular task instils it in our lives. You may even wish to write about the positives you have gained from a bad experience, which helps take the negative power from an issue, reminding us that every situation is multi-layered and, to see it properly for what it is, sometimes we need to look things from multiple perspectives.

SPIRITUAL TOOL: A DISPLAY OF THANKS AND CELEBRATION

Like the altar I have mentioned creating on our bedside table, we can also decorate our dining table with a particular theme. Taking the wheel of the year as a starting point, set out a display in the centre of the table which reflects the season. If you do not have enough space for this, then a windowsill or side table would work – you just need it to be somewhere you will see on a daily basis. Like the nature table you may have had at school or the decorating you do at Christmas, try collecting natural elements that echo the time of year, along with candles and any other items that celebrate the season we are in, and give thanks for the abundance around us.

Here is some seasonal inspiration to get you started:

- **Imbolc**, on 1 February, is midway between the winter solstice and the spring equinox. Burn candles to signify light returning and bring in foliage from outside to hint at the forthcoming spring. Add a bunch of snowdrops or hellebores. You could even take a kitsch approach and include woodland creature figurines found in a charity shop.
- **Summer Solstice**, around 21 June, means long days of light. Fill a vase with wildflowers like cow parsley, set crystals out for solstice intentions and add shells and pebbles for a summery beach theme.
- **All Hallows' Eve**, on 31 October, marks the time in the year when the veil between the living and the dead is at its thinnest. Put a tealight in a glass jar next to the photo of someone you have lost or place small pumpkins or squash on the table to signify the end of the harvest.

A good deed

A good deed can be for someone you already know, or it could be for a complete stranger. Maybe a friend is without their car for a few days and you offer them a lift, or they have just come out of hospital, so you pop round with some groceries – or, better still, a home-cooked meal. Maybe you have an elderly neighbour who doesn't get out very often and would love a cup of tea and a chat. You don't have to consider doing something big or time-consuming for someone, just a caring gesture to show you are thinking about them. **Selfless acts promote a feeling of wellbeing for the giver as well as the receiver**, as long as we don't keep score of them or do them for the sake of appreciation. This is not about one good turn deserving another.

There is a *Big Issue* seller outside my friend's local supermarket. She will often say hello to him and occasionally buys a magazine. Once, she was ahead of him in the queue for a takeaway sandwich in the café, and she said to the owner quietly that she would like to pay for his lunch as well as her own. The owner smiled and said she was very welcome to; they only charged him half price, so that is what they would charge her. They were two people, coming together in a moment, in a kind and respectful act. The café owner told the *Big Issue* seller, and he was grateful, but my friend didn't stick around for too long as she didn't want him to feel uncomfortable. She didn't do it for his thanks; it was about her appreciation of him for standing in all weathers and politely passing the time of day with her when she didn't buy a magazine. She did it in celebration and gratitude for human connection.

∞

Gratitude isn't a given

Not everyone can embrace gratitude as we are learning to, so it is a waste of energy to get cross with them when they don't. My client Sam spent an eternity waiting for appreciation from his boss. While he did not require thanks for doing a job he was being paid to do, he hoped to be thanked for those times he had gone above and beyond his professional commitments. He resented the lack of acknowledgement and began to scale back on the extra work he was doing. Eventually Sam's boss noticed his attitude had changed, but it was too late by then and Sam had found a new job. There are lessons on both sides. Sam couldn't expect gratitude and resent the lack of it without voicing how he felt, and his boss couldn't treat his staff in that way and expect them to stick around. All it would have taken was the occasional thank you, but Sam knew his boss wasn't able to give that and if that was what he needed he had to look elsewhere rather than sit in his resentment. Gratitude from others may not be important to you, but if it is, then find those who are able to give it and remember this works both ways.

SPIRITUAL TOOL: CEREMONIES OF GRATITUDE

There are rituals which are less regular but carry a huge significance, and the culmination of them can become a ceremony. While this can be a private, intimate experience, it is usually a more public declaration, like a shared event that gives us the opportunity to celebrate or commemorate something. Here are some you may want to try:

Thanksgiving Feast:

Thanksgiving is celebrated in October in Canada and November in America. Inviting people over for a Thanksgiving dinner could also be a lovely reason for you to gather loved ones around and thank them for being in your life. It's likely they will also want to show their appreciation for you, so invite them to bring a dish to add to the table if they want. Choosing the official Thanksgiving date gives a feeling of community as others also congregate, but if this feels too much like piggybacking on someone else's tradition, then arrange it for another day.

Gratitude Ritual:

Another opportunity to give thanks with friends, a gratitude ritual is a self-designed fire ceremony incorporating affirmations and reflection. This could be held around an altar table of candles and significant items, outside around a bonfire, or indoors in a semi-circle around a fireplace. Take it in turns to share your blessings as affirmations or write them down on pieces of paper before burning them and sending the grateful smoke into the universe. You may even want to summon your inner goddess to bear witness. Take a moment here for personal thought and thanks.

Cacao Ceremony:

A Cacao Ceremony is an ancient drinking ritual which recognises and gives thanks for the sacred natural world, its spirits and elements. Cacao is the rawest form of chocolate, full of minerals and antioxidants, which is turned into an unprocessed and unsweetened drink. Taking it need not be a ceremony for anyone else but you, although it is a lovely thing to share with others as a performance of long-held mystical tradition.

Ceremonial cacao comes from whole organic beans found in the wild which have been through a simple, traditional process to activate important compounds before being roasted, ground and blessed. This is a method which is steeped in intention, gratitude and respect from the moment the cacao is harvested under the protection of the sacred and wise Cacao Spirit, right through to the making of the product. You can order it online, and I would recommend taking time to choose one which speaks to you, whether it is from a particular area or has a story attached to it that resonates with you. (One small note of caution is to check whether you are unable to drink ceremonial cacao for any medical reasons, including epilepsy, heart issues or high blood pressure, or if you are taking anti-depressants.)

Make your ceremonial cacao with milk or a dairy-free alternative and add any spices, like cinnamon and ginger, and sweeteners such as honey or maple syrup.

As you do, consider the intentions and gratitude you may wish to share with yourself or others and thank the cacao as you make it. Take it to a space you have prepared or consider sacred. Light a candle and connect to the Cacao Spirit, beginning with gratitude to the cacao and the place it flourished. Now reflect on the challenges the environment faces, the journey the cacao took to get to you, and the people who were part of the process, before you give thanks for the abundance and harmony of life. Open your heart, be ready to receive, be humble in your intentions and surrender to the cacao for a deep, spiritual experience. You may choose to call your inner goddess at this point or give thanks to her, as in the Gratitude Ritual above. Some people say that she is there in the bubbles that start to form as the liquid warms up. As you sip the drink, you can meditate or visualise a specific goal or intention you have in mind. You could burn sage and send the smoke out to the universe, carrying your thanks before you set an intention down on paper.

A group ceremony follows a similar structure and is popular on yoga and mindfulness retreats as a way for us to connect more deeply with others, share our intentions and tap into the power of the gathering. It opens us up to others, ourselves and the universe.

This is as good as it gets

Sometimes gratitude emerges from our subconscious and we don't take the time to bask in it. Be alert, and when you feel that delicious tug in your tummy or find your mouth turning into a smile, acknowledge it. An extra tight hug with a loved one. A surprise visit from a dear friend. Catching a beautiful sunrise or sunset. Picking vegetables and flowers from the garden. The smell of a cake baking in the oven. **It's not always the big moments that matter; it is the countless tiny happenings that shine our soul.** An intentional life is a full, authentic, thankful one.

THE ENERGY OF PINK

Crystal: Rose quartz is the crystal for this chapter. Improving emotional wellbeing, opening the heart to give and receive gratitude, bolstering self-worth and encouraging spiritual wisdom, it is the stone of unconditional love. Keep it in your pocket or tuck it somewhere close.

Colour: Pink is also considered the colour of gratitude, and pink roses represent this in the flower world.

Affirmation:

I appreciate everything I have.

Journal Prompt: What eight things am I grateful for? How can I show my gratitude to someone close to me?

∞

This isn't the end. It's the beginning.

From building confidence, trusting your intuition, setting boundaries and pushing your potential to welcoming your inner goddess, finding time to rest, learning to love yourself and giving thanks, you have taken eight big steps towards a more intentional life. I am proud of how far we have come and excited for what is waiting ahead of you.

I sincerely hope that the questions I posed at the beginning of our quest, and those I raised throughout, have given you an opportunity to think more deeply about what you want from your wonderful life. Dip back into these pages whenever you need to and embed your favourite exercises into your weekly routine.

Like the symbol on the front of this book, my journey has carried its own infinity, and I wish you the same. Find your flow, one that continues to inspire, delight and connect you to those you love.

I have saved one final mantra for this moment. During those times when you feel yourself falling back into old habits, questioning your abilities and losing touch with your gut instinct or inner goddess, repeat this:

'Stop, assess, change.'

I have every faith in you. Be happy.

JAYNE'S SPIRITUAL KIT BAG

On being psychic

I have always felt like I am on a different frequency to other people. Not that I am special, but that my senses are highly attuned. I have strong taste buds, am susceptible to sound and I sometimes get a buzzing at the back of my head for no reason. Then there is my spiritual sixth sense, which has been with me from childhood. It is a gift I have always treasured and protected, other than a few teenage years in the self-imposed wilderness when I renounced my spirit guides and shut down the lines of communication. After my mum's death, my ability became my saviour and my life's work. I don't think I had any choice in the matter. Fate has always been good to me.

I know many people are curious about the spirit world, some are doubtful or disbelievers, and there are a few who are openly contemptuous, but I accept whatever reaction I receive. Everyone has their own beliefs, and I would never want to preach or try to convert people. I can only speak from my own understanding and experiences. Though some people may be born with psychic abilities, anybody can become psychic by training their mind, practising meditation, and developing their intuition. You have to be open to it. I am often asked what being psychic means to me.

In simple terms, as a psychic I connect to the spirit world and dead loved ones who have a message to share, acting as a conduit between this world and the next. I rely on my spirit guides, my intuition and all my senses as well as insightful tools like tarot and crystals. I have noticed a wider interest in what I do in recent years and many of my clients rely on our sessions for regular support and guidance. It can give them perspective, clarity and direction in areas like career, relationships, health, the future, dreams and desires. Some clients will turn to this in conjunction with psychotherapy in a bid to understand themselves better.

I love what I do and, for the most part, I have found a balance in my life between myself and my ability. As I head to work, I will open myself up to the spirits and feel my reading guides around me ready to connect with whoever my client brings with them from the spirit world. Within minutes, I will know whether I can get a connection or not. It rarely happens, but if I cannot pick up anything I flag this immediately. I do the same if the spirit they arrive with carries negative energy or is a psychic drain, and I tell my client I am shielding myself from this. At the end of the working day, I close down those lines of communication and put my protective shield up. Going home doesn't mean I stop being psychic, I am just very good at switching it off when I need a break.

I use tarot for readings depending on the client and the direction the session is heading in, and I will often pick up the cards without thinking. I know some psychics won't allow anyone to touch their tarot cards, but I encourage people to get involved, select cards and add their energy to the reading. I have my own themed decks of cards which I often turn to, covering the Major Arcana, which is all the big life stuff, and Minor Arcana for emotions and the everyday. I will shuffle the cards before inviting my client to pick six or nine depending on the type of reading we need to do and then lay them out, giving my interpretation. This is a great way to see issues and possible answers set out in front of you as well as gaining a truthful emotional response to possibilities and predictions.

If you have always wanted to visit a psychic, but have not yet done so, then there are several reasons why I would encourage you:

- If you are struggling to make a decision in significant areas of your life. A reading could throw new light and clarity on things, or give you a deeper understanding of what you want and check you are on the right path.

- If you want to connect to a dead loved one. Although there is no guarantee that it will be them who comes through, and it could be someone you do not expect, so be mindful of this.

- If you are spiritually curious and want to learn more.

Once you have made the decision to have a reading, do some research into reputable, trusted psychics who specialise in the area you feel most comfortable with, whether that is tarot, palm or aura. Psychic abilities vary widely, including clairvoyance (clear seeing), clairaudience (clear hearing), clairsentience (clear feeling) and mediumship (communicating with spirits). You should find reviews about them online or on social media or seek recommendations. Think about what you want from the experience and whether there are any questions you want to ask or issues you need clarity on. Being prepared and setting your intentions before the session means you can keep it on track and get the best from the experience.

As you prepare to go in, practise a deep breathing exercise and empty your mind of the day-to-day stuff and any distractions. This is your time, just as it would be if you were going for a therapy session or a massage. When a client arrives, I ask them if there are specific areas they want to look at and suggest saving all the detailed questions for the end of the session. Be open to what will come from the reading. Very occasionally someone will try to catch me out by remaining buttoned up or resisting the experience in some way and they only result in negatively impacting the experience for themselves.

This brings me to a word of caution. Sometimes people expect miracles from psychics. They long to connect with loved ones on the other side and when this doesn't happen, they are understandably bereft. Some assume we will have the answers to life and death. My role is to engender perspective, insight and strength, not to solve things, and I can only give what I get from the spirit world. Like the time I did a reading for a client and both her parents came through strongly. 'But where is my sister?' she wanted to know. She was happy to receive messages from her mum and dad, but it was her sister she wanted to hear from, and she was frustrated with me. Why couldn't I summon her? It was a difficult moment, and I told her I was not going to pretend to have a message from her sister when she simply wasn't there. 'Not there in life for me and now not there in death,' the client responded angrily. I think that was her answer; she didn't need me to explain this. Another time a client listened impatiently while I told her I had a message from her mother. 'I am not interested in hearing from her,' she said agitatedly. 'I want to hear from my dog.'

When you go for a reading, there is the possibility you will not like or agree with what you hear, so be prepared to be surprised by what may come up. Many years ago, I did a reading for a mate of mine, Annie. In hindsight, it was a mistake to do this for a friend and I should have passed her on to one of my colleagues. Her grandad came through in spirit and told me that Annie's husband was having an affair. I told her this and she refused to believe me, thinking I was trying to break up her marriage. I was clear that I only shared what I was given and maybe I should have ignored this message, but to do that would have been disrespectful to the spirit. If someone living or dead gives me a message to pass on to somebody else, then that is what I do. My friendship with Annie imploded that day and it was several years before I heard from her again. When she got back in touch, it was to say that I had been right, and she had left her husband.

At the beginning of a session, a client may want to focus on one particular aspect of their lives due to an issue they're having. By the end of the session, it can become clear the real focus should be on a different area that they hadn't considered before. This is part of the process and we need to trust in it.

If visiting a psychic is something you are going to explore, I truly hope it works for you and you gain a deeper insight into your life and your desires.

On tarot cards

I love doing tarot readings and my card packs are like my babies. I have different decks depending on who I may be reading for, what mood I am in, where the moon is in her cycle, which illustrations I am drawn to or what pack calls to me. That's the wonderful thing about tarot – it is universal, forgiving, welcoming, genuine and bursting with divine power. Many psychics will work with cards, but you don't have to go for a reading, because it is something you can do yourself. Everyone has a psychic ability they can tune into and using tarot cards is a great way to open this up, with a little patience and practice.

Begin by picking a deck that speaks to you. Working with tarot is a personal, intimate process and relies on your own interpretation, so it's important that you click with the cards. It can give in-depth insight and occasional harsh truths, which is why some people steer clear of it. Before you start, wrap your cards in something silk if you can and sleep with them under your pillow for a week to cleanse them from any previous touch and infuse them with your personal energy. After this time, pull out a card each day, study it and read what the information booklet tells you, but also draw your own conclusions about how you feel when you look at the card and hold it. Make friends with each card over the next couple of weeks.

When you are ready, there are various spreads you can try, so I have included my suggestions below. One note to be mindful of is to avoid reading your own tarot cards when you are feeling low. This is because it may affect your judgement when reading them and cause you to spiral further, which can be dangerous – quite the opposite to the intended effect.

Create the right environment for your tarot reading. Make sure you are somewhere quiet and relaxing, and that you won't be interrupted. You can even burn a sage stick to cleanse your space before you begin.

Shuffling the deck is a meditative process in itself and will ground, focus and help connect you to your spiritual self. As you do it, call on your intuition, your spirit guide or divine energy to be with you. Think about a specific question you may want to ask the cards as you do so. Some readers will shuffle and deal with the left hand because it is thought the energy channelled on that side of the body is linked to intuition and femininity and they will get a more in-depth result. My personal feeling is that it doesn't matter how you shuffle the cards, as long as you do so with intention. Here are some different card spreads that you can try:

THE THREE-CARD SPREAD

This is a really good place to start as a beginner, but it is also a spread I use regularly because it gives a simple, speedy response. Think of the question you want to ask and say it out loud to the cards as you divide your pack into three piles and set them next to each other. Turn over the top card on each of the piles and study what you have drawn.

Going from left to right, you can read them as:

1. The past (a particular event you are struggling to come to terms with)

2. The present (the challenge currently presented by this issue)

3. The future (how this situation will progress)

Or instead:

1. Situation (what the issue is)

2. Obstacle (what is in your way)

3. Advice (how to deal with the situation)

Each of these cards is giving you multiple messages, so take your time to focus on each one and use your intuition to understand its meaning. Once you have done this you can refer to the explanation handbook that you should have been given with the cards, which will explain them in more depth. While each of the cards is important, you are also looking at the overall message. It is useful to make a note of this reading to refer back to when you do this again in the future. It is a great way to chart change and progress.

THE SIX-CARD SPREAD

This is a step up from the three-card spread and, while still easy to read, it gives deeper insight and builds on our spiritual understanding. I would recommend you move on to this spread only once you feel confident working with three cards.

As before, shuffle your deck while thinking or saying aloud the question you want to ask and then split the deck into three piles. Working from left to right, turn over the first card and lay it on the pile. Let's call this card A. Take a card from the bottom of this pile and lay it below. Let's call this card AA. So you have taken out two cards from the top and bottom of the pack. Do the same with the remaining piles.

> **Stack A:** the two cards pulled from this are telling us what the heart of our issue is.
>
> **Stack B:** these two cards show how this situation will develop.
>
> **Stack C:** these two cards indicate a change or resolution.

Now look at the cards that sit on top of the pack (A, B, C), which represent your logical external world, then the cards that sit underneath (AA, BB, CC), which tell of an internal emotional reaction. Finally, you can read the cards across, taking cards A, BB and C to determine how your unconscious will work towards resolution, followed by cards AA, B and CC, which indicate the rational affecting the emotional.

THE NINE-CARD SPREAD

Traditionally set up as a 3x3 grid, this spread centres around the middle card and there are multiple ways to interpret the rest, so this is a more complicated one to work with. Whether the corners are context, or the top row is what's ahead/what we aim for and the bottom row is our current situation/circumstances leading to this moment, this can change from reader to reader. Once you are at this stage, I would suggest doing some research to find out what would work for you. I don't use this spread very often because my go-to is the Celtic Cross.

THE CELTIC CROSS

Whether you love it or hate it, this is considered to be the most famous of all tarot spreads and while there is a specific layout I use, there are others. Lay the cards out, picture-side down, and then turn each one over as you read.

Card 1: placed in the centre, this is your current obstacle, concern or mood.

Card 2: put this on top of card 1. This is the problem or challenge.

Card 3: to the left of these cards, put the next, representing the past.

Card 4: on the right of card 1 and 2, put the next, which depicts the future, either imminently or within a few months.

Card 5: place this above the middle cards. This shows us possibilities and aspirations.

Card 6: this card goes below the middle two and indicates our emotional, subconscious feelings and reactions.

Next, along the side of the cross, place the following cards in a vertical line from bottom to top:

Card 7: a card which offers advice and insight into the issue.

Card 8: a card to show what is beyond our control in this situation.

Card 9: this card will indicate hopes and fears and is trickier to decipher, so you may wish to pull another card to accompany it.

Card 10: the answer card, showing an outcome.

On spirit guides and why they matter

Throughout this book I ask you to call upon several spiritual entities, and I know how confusing this can be when you are taking tentative steps into a new understanding. The central characters in our quest for a more intentional life are our spirit guides, angels and inner goddess, and each fulfils a different brief and need. Here I want to talk about the importance of a spirit guide, introduce you to mine and help you to discover your own.

The first time I was aware of a spirit guide was when I encountered a figure who used to come into my dreams when I was little. Similar to the hooded shape of Death in a pack of tarot cards, this entity reminded me of the cartoon character Skeletor. Even though I couldn't see his face, I could sense he was staring at me and would wake up from those frightening dreams full of a foreboding I couldn't explain. When I told my mum, she told me the figure was my gatekeeper: the spirit that would follow me throughout life and be my connection between this world and the next. He was my protector. I tried to accept him as a positive force but that didn't stop me from being afraid of him. He must have known I was uncomfortable because he soon transformed into a young girl with the shape of a star on her forehead, which is why I gave her the name Star. She is still with me all these years later as my gatekeeper and is one of my channels to the spirit world. She keeps everyone in check and is able to close the channel if it becomes too much, protecting me from negative energy and deflecting bad spirits. I trust her implicitly.

This is my way to connect: I breathe in, sense the vibrations, use my mind's eye and call upon my guardian angels, my spirit guides (including Star) and my spiritual loved ones to come through. It's a collaborative effort, a bit like being in a conference call, and I ask them for support for different things. For instance, if I am about to do a healing, I will call upon my healing guide to assist me, and if I am linking to a lost loved one, I turn to my dad for guidance. Sometimes I am not in control of this. At a recent reading, my brother-in-law, who had taken his own life, came to me unbidden. He assisted me in the conversation with my client's dead brother who had also died by suicide.

When I'm doing a session with a client, my guides and intuition will make contact with the guides who have come in with them. My client will not be aware of their presence and they could be the spirit of a loved one. I will begin to receive messages which may come from our guides talking – this could be a vision, a physical feeling, overactive senses or a powerful energy. If I am healing, I may channel the client's ancestors, one male and one female at each shoulder, with whoever my client brings with them from the spirit world. That is the only time I do not ask who the spirits are, and instead focus on the healing. At the end of the day, as I head home, I slowly close them down, and when I go to bed at night, I will do a short meditation and thank them for their service and support. They need this acknowledgement and respect; it is a two-way relationship and a connection not to be abused.

It is hard to teach someone how to contact their spirit guides because it is such a personal experience, but I do have some useful tips to share. You need to be open to their particular energy through breathwork, meditation and visualisation. Meditation is one of the best ways to connect with your own spirit guides and request their help and assistance. It is likely that your spirit team is waiting in the wings, ready for you, and they will change as you grow.

Coupled with our intuition and senses, this is an ideal beginning. You may have a feeling of another entity around you, a little coldness perhaps, or an aura of colour. Why not ask them questions? What do they look like? What are they wearing? What is their name? The answers may appear in your head as if out of nowhere. They could be someone from another century or a different culture. Or they could be a loved one. Imagine you are a detective, piecing clues together. You may not be able to do this in one sitting but come back to it with the information you already have and see what more you can discover.

Now, when I need Star, all I have to do is call to her, visualise her in front of me and then she is there. Guides will change depending on what I need; there may be multiple coming and going, sometimes staying for a few weeks or longer. Star is the only constant. My dad is with me often, but my mum rarely visits, and my brother never has. I imagine this is because they are busy and happy and don't feel the need to return or have moved on to a new realm.

I was coming back from LA about eight years ago and, as I got on the plane, I could sense my mum. She was right there, in my mind's eye, every one of my senses working overtime to try to make her clearer and to hold on to her. Lee was talking to me, and I told him to stop. I needed to focus fully on my mum, and she was with me for the entire ten-hour flight. It was exhilarating and exhausting at the same time, but we had the biggest conversation up in the clouds.

Sometimes we have earth angels. Natalie is mine. She is one of the Psychic Sisterhood and is my real-life spirit guide. There is a real purity and strength to our connection. I know I can go to her about spiritual matters and she will listen, empathise and provide sage advice. If you do not feel ready to meet your spirit guides, then finding someone who personifies this for you in this world is a positive start. Again, as with the spirits, it is not a forced connection but a gut instinct about someone you know you can trust. These relationships are invaluable and act as mutually beneficial, beautiful support systems. For me, this defines the idea of the soulmate.

On the magic of angels

Guardian angels, the ethereal beings assigned to each of us from the day we are born, tread lightly in our shadow throughout our time on earth. They have never taken human form so are not subject to the frailties of ego, bias and change that can come with a spirit guide. Their energy is pure, light and freeing and their task is to help us achieve our personal mission and encourage us to rise above the difficulties in life and onto a pathway towards enlightenment.

Reaching out to our guardian angel for the first time can be daunting. When we connect with our spirit guide, we know who we are dealing with and we can picture them or sense their energy, but our angels are harder to imagine. In simple terms, our guardian angel is there to ask for help, to focus us on our emotions and gut instincts, and to help us trust that this will give us an answer to our conflict. In order to do this, we also need to be aware of our surroundings and be ready for the messages our guardian angel will send us.

Once we have faith in their existence, meditation is a great way to build a relationship, helping us to be open to receive visions and images from our angel speaking directly to us. As you search within yourself for answers, be alert to repetitive thoughts that appear unbidden, as they could be a response from your angel. Trust in the messages they bring, as they would never put you in a place of harm or ask you to do something you are uncomfortable with.

SIGNS FROM YOUR GUARDIAN ANGEL

The appearance of signs and how we recognise them is a personal choice. Feathers are a universal sign of an angel being near and I will always pick one up when I see it. For me, a robin also represents my angel, but it may be different for you. I know some people recognise their angel in a certain word which may pop up, a vivid dream or a familiar smell that acts as a message of love and reassurance. Alternatively, if you are struggling with something particular, then you can choose a sign for that moment.

A client of mine, Chloe, was making a difficult decision in her career and I suggested she ask for a sign from her guardian angel. Without thinking, an image of a frog popped into her head, and she took that as a message from her angel. She knew, if she saw a frog within the next twenty-four hours, this would support the decision she was making. The following day, the thought of a frog furthest from her mind, she was walking to the Tube and she found herself drawn to a gift shop she hadn't taken notice of before. She had never been inside, but something was pulling her towards the window, and there, in the centre of the display, was a large ceramic frog. We both felt this was a sign that changing direction in her work life was the right choice, and this has proved to be the case.

ANGEL NUMBERS

You may find you are seeing the same sequence of numbers on a regular basis, perhaps looking at your phone as the time reads 11:11 or being aware of a single number everywhere you go. This is not a coincidence and could be your angel communicating with you, so stay tuned in to the world around you, fire up your intuition and take the time to think about how your thoughts and feelings connect with these number appearances. There might be a pattern to this, or a repetitive sequence of numbers which keep cropping up, showing that your angel is present and ready to help you navigate on your journey.

How we read these numbers can be by personal definition, or you may find it helpful to follow a trusted guide. I have established my own explanations as well as combining with more widely used definitions. Here is the plan I created for myself, with a little help from other influences. You are welcome to use this when you see a sequence of numbers repeated, but I would also recommend that you take a moment to pause and reflect on how you're feeling. Are you happy or sad, confused or contented? Looking inwards will give you a sense of what this number means to you and what your angel may want to convey. Over time, you can develop your own method for interpreting your angel numbers, but try my interpretations below to begin with.

0 – A sequence of three or four is a direct message of support from your angel and could herald a fresh start. Why not make a wish when you see this appear?

1 – A manifestation number. When this is repeated, it is considered one of the most powerful sequences and tells us to engage with the universe for its support. You could visualise something you want to happen and trust in your angel's support.

2 – A sequence of twos, e.g. 222, is a master number and indicates an imbalance as well as a need to be more open to love.

3 – Three is one of the most mystical and creative numbers. 333 speaks of spirituality, magical growth and divine power.

4 – This sequence can signify balance and the ability to face things head on. Your angel will be there to help you.

5 – I love 555 or 5555 because it reassures me change is on its way. If you are stuck in a rut and unsure how to move on, seeing this number will tell you transformation is imminent as your angel works to bring it to fruition.

6 – As a repetitive number, six has been associated with the devil, but this sequence is a reminder to question our perspective, listen to our intuition and be kind to ourselves.

7 – A number that highlights a need to realign our values and encourage abundance, particularly in financial matters.

8 – This can signify a big chapter in life is coming to a close and we need to accept that and move on. It is also the infinity sign, upended, showing flow and also connecting to us the spirit world.

9 – A number that encourages us to step boldly and faithfully into the unknown. Use it to visualise the next part of your journey

On working with chakras

An ancient philosophy originating in India and part of the spiritual traditions of Hinduism and Buddhism, the word chakra means 'wheel' in Sanskrit, an ancient language of South Asia, and describes the power of each of the positions on the body which connect to create a map of our psychic energies. There are seven main chakras and these are positioned in a vertical line down our body: the crown of the head, third eye, throat, heart, solar plexus, sacral and root. Chakras are thought to be closely intertwined with our nervous system and have a direct correlation with our mental and physical sense of wellbeing. Chakras need to stay in sync and balanced in order for our mind and body to function at their best, and should be kept 'open' so as not to disrupt our energy flow. If a chakra is 'blocked' or not functioning optimally, then negative physical and emotional symptoms associated with that chakra can develop.

Chakras can get blocked during times of prolonged stress or unhealthy habits, and if you feel like you are spiralling, this can undermine your ability to function at your best. It only takes one blocked disc to upset our whole flow of energy. One way of dealing with this is through the ancient and spiritual practice of yoga, which can restore the energy in our bodies and isolate individual chakras to address the issues. Yoga is so much more than just exercise. Through poses, breathwork and focus, it promotes balance, flexibility and strength, emotionally as well as physically. In the last couple of decades there has been an explosion of popularity for various types of yoga, including Hatha (gentle movements so ideal for beginners), Ashtanga (a strenuous approach), Bikram (referred to as hot yoga because of the temperature you practise it at) and Vinyasa (which flows from one stance to the next).

Alternatively, if, like me, you can't do yoga for health or other reasons, you can deal with your chakras through meditation instead.

THE SEVEN MAIN CHAKRAS

Crown

Located at the top of the head

Colour of violet

Indicates awareness, intelligence, spirituality

Third Eye

Located between the eyes on the forehead

Colour of indigo

Indicates imagination and intuition

Throat

Located in the throat

Colour of blue

Indicates communication

Heart

Located in the centre of the chest

Colour of green

Indicates love and compassion

Solar Plexus

Located in the upper abdomen

Colour of yellow

Indicates self-esteem and confidence

Sacral

Located midway between the navel and the pubic bone

Colour of orange

Indicates sexuality, pleasure and creativity

Root

Located at the base of the spine

Colour of red

Indicates identity, stability and grounding

On meditation

Like chakras, meditation originated in India thousands of years ago before being adopted by various belief systems and different cultures, creating countless practices for us to experience today. Meditation is a valuable tool which can help in many ways, including to improve our focus, lower stress, stay calmer, quieten the busyness in our heads and understand our thoughts better.

A patience-driven exercise, it is simple to do but requires regular and consistent practice. It is surprising how quickly our mind will wander, and as much as we pull it back into focus, it can slip off again. One of the first things is to tackle our breathing, and by concentrating on this we can take the first step into meditative practice.

There are various ways to access meditation:

- **Mindfulness:** Concentrate on the thoughts and images that float into your head before gently dismissing them.

- **Spirituality:** Saying a prayer or repeating a mantra, whether this is the classic repetitive sound 'ommmmm' or something else you feel comfortable with.

- **Focus:** Harnessing the five senses and placing yourself in your environment.

- **Movement:** This could be yoga, tai chi, walking in nature or gardening.

If this is not something you have done before, begin with a simple exercise. Set aside several minutes, sit somewhere quiet and make yourself comfortable. Close your eyes, inhale steadily through your nose for a few seconds, hold your breath for a moment and then slowly exhale through your mouth. Feel your breath and allow yourself to be in touch with your body, recognising where you are feeling any tension. It's important to relax your body and let go of any judgement. It doesn't matter if and where your mind wanders, but you should always bring it back to the present. If your mind is returning to a particular thought, perhaps take some time after your meditation to explore this further in your journal. Turning meditation into a regular habit ultimately makes us better at it and in turn it becomes a more effective tool to help us feel in touch with our minds and bodies. It is one of the most compelling and accessible practices I have included in this book.

On crystals and their properties

As you will know from the way I have structured this book and how I write about them, crystals are hugely important to me in every aspect of my life. I am never without them, and I rely on a variety of gemstones for different reasons. You'll have noticed that I have even given each chapter of this book its own specific crystal. The combination of all eight crystals that I have spoken about make a potent collection, but you don't have to stop there or even choose the ones I highlight. If this is the beginning of your spiritual journey, you may prefer to start with one or two to avoid being overwhelmed.

Like us humans, crystals hold energies that can be incredibly powerful when combined with our own. Crystals help with the flow of good energy while cleansing us of negative vibrations and promoting physical, emotional and spiritual wellbeing. They instil tranquillity, positivity, balance and focus and can also act as a talisman in difficult situations.

By having them near us, wearing them or sleeping with them under our pillow, we can receive all kinds of benefits depending on the crystal's properties, whether it be comfort, protection or a feeling of reinvigoration. This practice, rooted in ancient tradition, makes them a vital part of our spiritual toolkit. In truth, I don't think I could function properly without them.

When you are choosing crystals, you may prefer not to refer to external information and instead make your decision based on a stone you are drawn to. Let your intuition do the work to select the appropriate crystal and allow your energy to connect to the power it emits. You may think you have been seduced by its look or colour, but it's just as likely that the crystal chose you.

If you would prefer a helping hand with your crystal choice, I have included a list of the central gemstones below. Pick a crystal that you feel can help to enhance your life or support you in an area where you may be struggling. Some crystals work together as a pair – like amethyst and rose quartz for helping to promote strength and reduce anxiety, and fluorite and clear quartz to aid concentration and focus – so you may feel like you would benefit from bringing specific crystals together. As a general rule, crystal properties are colour-based, with dark colours assigned to individual protection, such as brown for cleansing and green for calm. Lighter colours are associated with purity, such as pink for love and red for energy.

Before you begin to work with your crystals, you will need to cleanse them of any energies they may have picked up before they found their way to you. Some can be washed in water, but not all should be treated in this way, so do check this before you submerge them. It is also important to cleanse crystals at least once a month, as they absorb negative energy and could hold on to stagnant or misdirected vibrations. Turn this into a ritual which will benefit you also. Here are various methods you could use:

- Utilise the divine magic of a full moon by putting your crystals on a windowsill or outside to recharge them.

- When it rains, put your crystals outside to cleanse them or immerse them in a bowl of cold salt water. If this is sea water, then even better!

- Use a sage stick to smudge them. Passing them quickly through the flame of a candle will also work.

- Dig a hole in the soil and bury your crystals for twenty-four hours, allowing the earth to absorb unwanted energy and cleanse and re-energise the crystals.

- Set your crystals down with a cleansing crystal. A selenite tower is an excellent way to clear the energy of other crystals.

CHOOSE YOUR CRYSTAL

Clear Quartz

A clear crystal associated with healing and energy. A 'master healer'. Often used in meditation and spiritual practice to set intentions and manifest desires.

Amethyst

A purple stone that connects to the third eye and can enable me to reach my spirit guides. It gives a higher intuitive vibration and is associated with purity, humility and spiritual wisdom. It is also known for its calming properties, as it can help to soothe the mind and body. It is my go-to crystal and I often use it to help with my joint pain.

Lapis lazuli

This blue stone encourages us to use our voice and gives us the right words. It supports us in trusting ourselves, helps us to utilise our inner voice to communicate and gives us confidence to grow and evolve.

Green aventurine

The stone of the emotional heart and healing, it gives us the strength and courage to make positive changes in our lives.

Rose quartz

This crystal is focused on the heart and encapsulates trust and love in all its guises, including self-love. It encourages us to believe in who we are and comforts us through moments of stress and anxiety.

Citrine

The yellow crystal of abundance, structure and stability. It is also known as the stone of manifestation and helps us explore our creativity and boosts our concentration

Tiger's eye

A luxurious gold and brown, this is the stone of structure, giving grounding and stability. It helps us make clear, conscious decisions.

Red Jasper

The stone of passion, it promotes empowerment as well as support and nurture and inspires us to have confidence in everything we do.

Turquoise

This blue stone is known for its protection and guidance in friendships, and it encourages happiness within both ourselves and those around us.

Black obsidian

A crystal that helps to cleanse and clear the home of negative energy. Place on the windowsill as a shield of protection from external forces.

Black tourmaline

This stone brings balance into our lives, encouraging us to set and implement boundaries.

On spiritual healing

I am a big advocate for the transformative power of spiritual healing, which can get to the root of the emotional causes of stress and illness to bring balance and clarity. We can each take control of this for ourselves, through meditation, affirmation and mindfulness, as well as working with a recommended practitioner in various methods.

I work with holistic techniques including reiki, pranic healing, crystal therapy and shamanic rituals to cleanse spiritual energy. These practices are also known to alleviate chronic pain, heal trauma and promote spiritual awareness.

REIKI

Originating in Japan in the early twentieth century, reiki is a form of energy healing. It is a holistic practice rooted in the belief that an invisible 'life force energy' flows through all living things and keeps us balanced and healthy. When this is clogged or upset in some way, it has an emotional or physical impact. Reiki healers use the technique of the laying on of hands or placing them over the body to channel healing vibrations to reduce stress, aid relaxation and help the body's natural healing processes. A non-invasive approach, it can be used to target specific ailments as well as instilling a harmonious feeling of mental and physical wellbeing.

At the beginning of a reiki session, I will discuss areas a client is keen to focus on before moving my hands across their body and channelling healing energy to the points I feel are in need of it. This can create a deep sense of wellbeing, calm and balance as the healing vibrations travel through them. It also helps open psychic pathways to support a reading during or after the session, deepening the experience and giving greater insight.

I will often incorporate crystals in reiki treatments to harness their specialised energy during the healing process. Every crystal carries its own frequency, which can positively affect the body's energy to help clear blockages and enhance the power of reiki healing. These can be placed around or on the body, either focusing on places that need support or in alignment with chakras. The crystals I tend to use in this healing practice include amethyst, because of its ability to boost spiritual awareness and bring a welcome sense of calm; clear quartz, which is often referred to as the 'master healer'; and rose quartz for emotional healing, self-love and empathy. Black tourmaline is a protective stone which shields against negativity, and uplifting citrine manifests abundance.

PRANIC HEALING

This is an alternative hands-off practice which focuses on the cleansing of the body's energy to promote wellbeing. Life energy, known as prana, flows through us, and when it is adversely affected it can attack our physical and mental health. Working on the principle that our body is able to repair itself, it uses energy vibrations similar to reiki and may also include crystals.

CRYSTAL HEALING

As well as supporting the practices I have already mentioned, crystals can be the focus of healing sessions, using their unique energy to target specific areas on the body or follow the chakras.

CHAKRA HEALING

Chakra healing focuses on the seven main chakra points in the body to cleanse and clear our pathways and balance energy, through the use of meditation, visualisation and crystals. Refer back to page 219 for more information on chakras.

SHAMANIC HEALING

Shamanic healing is an ancient tradition where the healer enters a trance-like state to converse with the natural spirit world in order to treat emotional, mental and physical health. Shamans will also perform rituals and turn to medicinal plants and oils to cleanse negative energy and recover lost aspects of the soul. This is thought to be good for trauma.

SOUND HEALING

Sound frequencies can be used in the healing process for both physical and emotional issues. Sound healing involves instruments including gongs and singing bowls, which are used to create vibrations which aid relaxation and rejuvenation.

ON GODDESSES

Overleaf you will find a selection of goddesses from *The Mythic Goddess Tarot*, the deck I created. I have taken the text from the cards; as you will see, each goddess carries huge significance.

Rhiannon: Judgement

Meaning: Inner calling
Key words: Healing, change, focus, rebirth
Affirmation: *I am focused on the choices I make.*

Rhiannon reminds us that the truth can set us free, and that healing and second chances do happen. Time to discover spirituality and the best you. You are being offered another opportunity. Trust your own innate sense of what is right and wrong. Whatever hurt has been piled on, you are at a crossroads and need to make a choice or a judgement. What have past lessons taught you? It's time for wounds to be healed and for salvation. Forgiveness is a big theme of this card. Take a breath. Reach out to others and reassess the past. Use your inner judgement to work out which situations to leave behind forever and which deserve your time, energy and love.

Lakshmi: The World

Meaning: Achievement
Key words: Prosperity, ending, movement, new beginnings
Affirmation: *I am successful in everything I do.*

Lakshmi tells us that good fortune is possible with hard work and a little humility. A long-term project, relationship or career matter has come full circle and is revealing fulfilment. This can represent an engagement, birth, promotion or another kind of career goal which has been, or is about to be, reached. Travel may also be a part of your immediate future. This card represents achievement and satisfaction. You feel whole and complete, and you are enjoying your sense of accomplishment. Things are turning out how you wish. Yes, you have learned lessons on the way, but you have also enjoyed good fortune. Remember to be thankful and see how far you have come.

Magec: The Sun

Meaning: Joy

Key words: Emotional wealth, joy, confidence

Affirmation: *I am happy in myself and grounded in the world around me.*

Here comes the sunshine after a period of darkness! You can expect a boost in wellbeing and mood. If you've been waiting for matters to get better, start smiling! After some challenges, you are stepping into success and are full of energy and a zest for life. You're exuding confidence and, following the law of attraction, abundance is coming your way. Family life is blessed, and if you are planning to extend your brood, there could be good news for you. If you've had a disagreement with someone, reconciliations can happen now. Celebrations and vacations are beautifully starred by this card. Love and proposals are also possibilities.

Selene: The Moon

Meaning: Illusion

Key words: Intuition, uplifting, reflective

Affirmation: *I see the light through the darkness.*

Sometimes the moon is visible, at other times she disappears. However, she is always there. This is the message that is being bestowed by Selene. You feel like your inner knowledge has left you. But take heart and know it is present. There may be something in your life that is not as it seems, or perhaps your judgement is being distorted by emotional distress or long-buried memories. Selene is asking you to process the hurt. Try guided meditation, Shamanic healing, or hypnosis. It's about bypassing the rigid, structured part of your brain and accessing pure intuition. Something in your current situation isn't quite as it is being presented to you. When making big decisions, don't take things at face value. Dreams, intuition and inner guidance are your friends now. Selene is telling you to go deep and sleep on it. Then all will be clear.

Asase Yaa: The Empress

Meaning: Abundance

Key words: Motherhood, fertility, nurture, honesty

Affirmation: *I am grounded and surrounded by abundance.*

New beginnings and rebirth are on the horizon. Fertility is starred – this may be in the literal sense with a new baby. This card can also represent a new romance or venture. Like Asase Yaa, all you need to do is give a wish your touch and you may have a successful outcome. Express yourself creatively with arts, music and writing. Money and resources should become plentiful, and a house move may happen. A positive new relationship could be on the horizon. Good fortune surrounds this card, and you should feel that Asase Yaa is caring for and guiding you.

Elpis: The Star

Meaning: Hope

Key words: Dreams, ambition, belief

Affirmation: *I believe in everything I do.*

Whatever is happening to you in your life, allow yourself a smile. Even if you feel you have made a mistake, hope and healing are with you. You should find yourself feeling positive and serene, connected with spirits and looking towards new horizons. Elpis's presence indicates that you can heal. It's time for a spring in your step. There will be renewal and joy in relationships, money will start to flow again, and you will see the flicker of opportunity, which motivates and invigorates you.

Juno: The Hierophant

Meaning: Spiritual wisdom

Key words: Knowledge, companionship, customs, spirituality

Affirmation: *I am open to learning.*

Juno stands for tradition. She was celebrated throughout the traditional Roman calendar as the focus of several major festivals. Juno advocates looking at tried and tested ways of doing things as they could offer answers and protection. Perhaps family traditions have fallen by the wayside and your heart is yearning for them. Juno is also alerting you to opportunities. Is there someone around you who you respect, who you can learn from? A teacher, mentor or guide could be arriving in your life and offering structure and principles, or you could be joining a respected group or institution. Gaining knowledge and studying are highlighted by this card, as is serious relationship commitment.

Tyche: The Wheel of Fortune

Meaning: Destiny

Key words: Movement, luck, transformation

Affirmation: *I am moving freely.*

Tyche's presence signifies amazing good fortune. There can be marvellous encounters and lucky breaks when she is present. Tyche is urging you to grab chances and run with them and to build on good things. This will help bring more positivity and bounty into your life. Understand that luck is close, even if it doesn't feel that way. Tyche asks you to remember you can make your own good fortune too. Your intuition is highly developed, and it can lead you to opportunity. Wealth, in the form of promotions and pay rises, is possible, and Tyche is an excellent help with job hunting too. If you have your own business, you should find that success and prosperity are beckoning. Should you wish to move, this card suggests you may discover your dream home and love may blossom for single people.

Ma'at: The Emperor

Meaning: Authority

Key words: Legality, balance, justice, decisions

Affirmation: *I make my own decisions and trust my intuition.*

Ma'at represents a righteous moral code, which links with the divine and the soul, and leadership, fostering honour and discipline. A decision may be needed that requires you to act rationally, with integrity and for the greater good. Promotions, achievements and deserved accolades may be coming your way. You could be taking on a leadership role. You are clear-eyed when it comes to manifesting your goal and you have the strength to say and do what is right. Remember you are in charge, and you have the final say. You have the power and moral authority to settle disagreements now. In love, this card can represent being involved with someone who possesses great wisdom.

USEFUL DIRECTORY

Here are just a few of the amazing organisations which can further support the themes I have discussed in the book.

Spiritualists' National Union
Supports spiritualist churches and training
www.snu.org.uk

Samaritans
www.samaritans.org

Mind
Mental health support
www.mind.org.uk

The Arthur Findlay College
The college for the advancement of spiritualism and psychic sciences
www.arthurfindlaycollege.org

Alcoholics Anonymous

www.alcoholics-anonymous.org.uk

ACKNOWLEDGEMENTS

In keeping with my final chapter on embracing gratitude, there are several people I want to thank for working on this book because it wouldn't exist without them.

To my agent, Chelsey Fox, for guiding and advising me, and Lucy Brazier, for joining me on this writing journey.

To my lovely editor, Katy Follain, and her fab team at Bloomsbury, including Laura Cope, Victoria Denne and Fabrice Wilmann.

To Tracey Emin for her friendship, Sara Davies for her support and Kim Kardashian for her kind quote.

To my wonderful Psychic Sisters gang, both in Selfridges and the warehouse.

To all my friends and family for being the best and to my fiancé, Lee Ryan, for being the best of the best.

Lastly, to my spirit guides Star, my mum, my dad and brother Terry, for giving me spiritual guidance when I needed it the most. (Love and miss you.)

Thank you all.

A NOTE ON THE AUTHOR

Jayne Wallace is an internationally acclaimed wellness entrepreneur. She is the owner of the wellness brand Psychic Sisters, which is based in Selfridges, London, and featured on the BBC's *Dragons' Den* in 2023. Her work has featured in *Marie Claire*, *The New York Times*, *The New Statesman*, *OK Magazine*, *The Sun* and *The Mirror*. Jayne's high-profile celebrity clients include Tracey Emin, Kim Kardashian, Rita Ora, Kid Cudi and Kate Hudson, among many others. She is based in the UK.